TEXAS

An Illustrated History

TEXAS
AN ILLUSTRATED HISTORY

JOHN PERRY

HIPPOCRENE BOOKS, INC.
New York

Copyright © 2011 John Perry

All rights reserved.

For information, address:
HIPPOCRENE BOOKS, INC.
171 Madison Avenue
New York, NY 10016
www.hippocrenebooks.com

Library of Congress Cataloging-in-Publication Data

Perry, John, 1937-
  Texas : an illustrated history / John Perry.
      p. cm.
  ISBN-13: 978-0-7818-1266-5 (pbk.)
  ISBN-10: 0-7818-1266-6 (pbk.)
  1. Texas--History. 2. Texas--History--Pictorial works. I. Title.
  F386.6.P47 2011
  976.4--dc23
                                              2011022450

Printed in the United States of America

For Sweetie

Contents

I	Don't Mess with Texas	1
II	To Serve God and Get Rich	9
III	Come and Get It!	23
IV	Within the Sound of the Drum	35
V	A Rich Jewel Lying Derelict	53
VI	The Damndest Troops in the World	63
VII	The Wild Ravings of Fanatics	77
VIII	A Conquered Province	91
IX	Cowboys, Comanches, and Crooks	97
X	The New Gospel of Political Salvation	113
XI	Rigs of Prosperity	125
XII	Where the Chicken Got the Axe	139
XIII	The Business of America is Business	153
XIV	Gone To Texas	167
	Suggestions for Further Reading	179
	Photo Credits	183
	Index	185

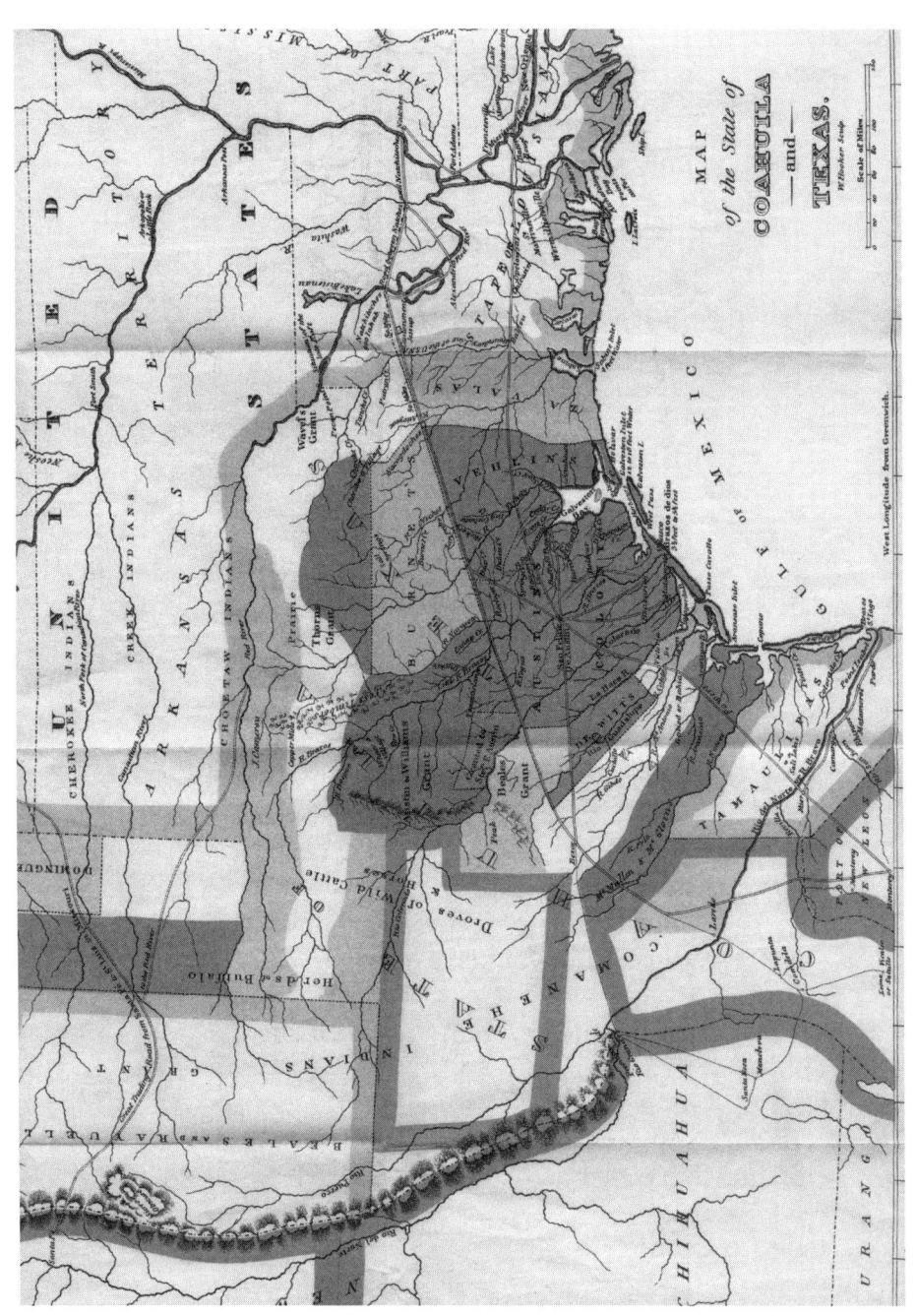

1830s map of the Spanish state of Coahuila-Texas

Chapter I

Don't Mess with Texas

"Land comes before anything else in Texas. Long before the first humans arrived, in a time when rivers only flowed toward the Gulf of Mexico without serving as political boundaries or arteries of commerce ... before people converted the open spaces to enclosures and claimed exclusive ownership and use of certain parts of the earth, before attitudes and morals and ethics and prejudice. Texas was just land."
—Archie P. McDonald, *In Celebration of Texas*

One word comes to mind when thinking about Texas. BIG! The state covers nearly 270,000 square miles with a population of nearly 25 million in 265 counties—second only to Alaska in size and California in population. It's five times bigger than England and twice the size of Japan. All of New England plus Ohio, Illinois, Pennsylvania, and New York could fit inside its borders. The state sprawls 350 miles along the Gulf of Mexico and almost 900 miles from Dalhart in the Panhandle to Brownsville on its southern tip. Texas also boasts three of the ten largest cities in the country: Houston, San Antonio, and Dallas. All this bigness helps explain why road signs in the state say: "Don't mess with Texas."

Because of the state's huge size—one-twelfth of the U.S.'s land area—it also has one of the country's most varied climates. This is caused in part by its many different landforms: plains, hills, forests, mountains, canyons, and deserts. Cold and snow aren't rare in the Panhandle. The Great Blizzard of 1886-87 blighted the cattle industry. In 1956, over thirty inches of snow fell on Amarillo. Cold, wet air masses known as "northers" also often hit the Panhandle and can move south to the Gulf coast—a far cry from the hot, humid weather usually associated with Texas that leaves one dripping. Temperatures reached 120 degrees at Seymour in 1936. Yet un-

Palo Duro Canyon

welcome droughts and thunderstorms can cause hail and flash flooding. Clarksville had nearly 110 inches of rain in 1873, while Wink in West Texas had about 2.0 inches in 1956, which made the ground crack like over-baked crockery. The San Antonio area suffered severe droughts from 2008-2011. Tornadoes and hurricanes also hit the state because it's on the edge of "Tornado Alley." One twister touched down in Wichita Falls in 1979. The 1900 Galveston hurricane was the worst in U.S. history—until Hurricane Katrina came along in 2005.

Many questions come to mind when looking at the geography of Texas. Why is it so big when the U.S. wanted to keep states pretty much the same size? And why does its shape sprawl in so many different directions when most other states are either square or rectangular? For example, the Panhandle in western Texas pushes into Oklahoma, leaving that state with a small section that looks like the handle of a meat chopper. Most borders of Texas also run in crooked lines. When Texas became a state in 1846, why did it give all its land above 36°30' to the U.S.—especially after fighting for it during the revolution? And why does its border turn north from the Red River at the 100th meridian?

Three rivers help shape Texas's boundaries. The Red River begins in New Mexico, flows nearly 1,400 miles, and separates Texas from Oklahoma. The Sabine River runs along the eastern edge of Texas, sometimes called the Piney Woods. And the Rio Grande starts in Colorado, winds along New Mexico, and forms a border between Texas and Mexico. Early travelers not only admired the land's waterways, but also its lush forests, vegetation, and climate.

Mary Austin Holley praised the area in *Texas: Observations, Historical, Geographical and Descriptive* (1833): "I am perfectly satisfied that Texas is, in many respects, the most eligible part of North America ... Its climate is salubrious, pleasant, and diversified, partaking of the tropical and the temperate ... It presents every species of soil that can be found in alluvion, level, undulating, or mountainous land, embracing all the varieties of clayey, sandy, pebbly, rocky, with all the intermixes. The state is sufficiently supplied with good timber and woodland, also with the most useful metals and fossils. Its harbors and rivers are well adapted to facilitate all the purposes of commercial intercourse both at home and abroad."

The anonymous *Visit to Texas* (1834) also remarked about the San Felipe area: "Surely no land could be found in any part of the world, where nature has done more to give the landscape the aspect of art ... No words can do justice to its peculiar appearance, or excite the feelings which we experienced in traveling in it, especially when we wandered, as we often did, through unmeasured fields of flowers, with nothing but the compass to dictate our course, while every thing seemed equally attractive on every side."

David B. Edward in his 1836 *History of Texas* extolled: "The province of Texas in general, for native beauty, and the lower division in particular for exuberant fecundity is excelled by no other country I have ever known." He also called San Antonio's site "one of the most beautiful in the western world."

The abundant natural regions of Texas haven't only changed over the past several hundred years, but have caused many quarrels and conflicts, both among its diverse natives and people from other countries. Barkley and Odintz say in *The Portable Handbook of Texas*: "The location of Texas boundaries has been the subject of international and interstate conflict resulting in treaties, litigation, and commissions from 1736 to the present." Its borders certainly support the belief that geography exerts a strong influence on culture.

Eastern Border

Why does the eastern border of Texas look like a saw blade? Blame it on the Sabine and Red Rivers. In 1819 the U.S. and Spain set national boundaries through the Adams-Onís Treaty. (John Quincy Adams was Secretary of State and Luis de Onís was the Spanish Minister in Washington.) The Red River became an issue during these negotiations because it flowed diagonally across Texas to the Mississippi River and was also important to Louisiana trade. The two countries finally drew a vertical line where the Sabine River crossed the 32nd parallel until it intersected the Red River above—although where the 32nd parallel crossed the Sabine River remained a mystery. Some people claimed Adams gave part of Louisiana to Texas, but the original capital of Spanish Texas, Los Adaes, stood east of the Sabine River.

The jagged line defined by the Red River continued west until it reached the 100th meridian, then turned north to the Arkansas River, a point that's now the eastern edge of the Texas Panhandle. Why the 100th meridian? Onís wrote Adams in early 1819: "I have to state to you that his majesty is unable to agree to [the boundary of] the Red River to its source, as proposed by you. This river rises within a few leagues of Santa Fe, the capital of [Spanish] New Mexico." So they selected the midpoint between the headwaters of the Arkansas River and Louisiana. In 1858, however, surveyors learned this line was off one hundred miles to the east. In 1896 the Supreme Court reset it at the Prairie Dog Town Fork of the

Red River. But in 1919 Oklahoma filed suit when oil was discovered in the bed of the Red River. So after much court wrangling, the line was changed once again. One Oklahoma woman remarked that she hadn't moved a foot in 45 years, yet had lived in a territory, two states, and three counties.

A few words on early Texas maps: Most were filled with inaccuracies. Thomas Jefferson didn't know how far southwest Louisiana extended until after the U.S. bought it from Napoleon in 1803. When Mexico declared its independence from Spain in 1821, one map called its northern regions "Unknown Country." This was also true of the Big Bend area on the western border of the state. An 1835 map only extended west to the Nueces River and called land north of the Red River "Santa Fe, formerly New Mexico." Travel guides likewise made mistakes because they plagiarized other maps. After Texas joined the U.S., its enormous size baffled the army, the Texas Rangers, and the General Land Office, leading to a law that required each county to hire a mapmaker. As late as 1904, the *Gazetteer of Texas* remarked that "the subdivision of Texas lands has not resulted in the production of maps of much value." All of this helps explain the Texas differences with Mexico and nearby states over determining borders during the 19th century.

NORTHERN BORDER

Before Texas declared independence in 1836, the northern border of Spanish Mexico followed the boundaries of the Adams-Onís Treaty. When Mexico won its independence from Spain, it continued the policy of discouraging American settlement, although Moses Austin talked the government into granting him land. Then Texas declared its independence from Mexico, got strapped for funds, and became part of the U.S. in 1846.

Texas needed slavery to keep its economic reliance on cotton and other agricultural products. But the Missouri Compromise (1820) declared slavery illegal north of the 30°36' parallel. (They called it the Missouri Compromise because when the U.S. admitted Missouri as a slave state, it also admitted Maine as a free state to keep a sectional balance.) To solve this problem, Texas politicians gave the Union all land north of that latitude, which created the Panhandle area. This section included parts of current-day Oklahoma, Kansas, Colorado, Wyoming, and New Mexico. It's ironic that Congress repealed the Missouri Compromise when it passed the Kansas-Nebraska Act, letting people in these territories make their own decisions about slavery. Then the Missouri Compromise was declared un-

The Rio Grande

constitutional in the 1857 Dred Scott decision. So this hasty action lost Texas lots of land.

SOUTHERN BORDER

The Rio Grande River (Rio Bravo del Norte in Mexico) runs along the entire border between Mexico and the U.S. This river has been the cause of much ill will and bloodshed between the two countries. The 1819 Adams-Onís Treaty between Spain and the U.S. stated that the U.S. ceded Texas to Spain and that the Sabine and Red Rivers would become the southern boundary of the Louisiana Purchase. But when Texas became independent in 1836, politicians changed this line to the Rio Grande, which Mexico never recognized. This helped inflame the Mexican War of 1846 after Texas joined the U.S. Following this clash, Mexico accepted the boundary, and the river became international waters—which aided Texas during the Civil War, when steamers floated a fortune in cotton down it to waiting English ships.

WESTERN BORDER

The U.S. Congress believed that all states should be created equal—but enormous Texas even spilled over into current-day New Mexico. This so concerned Congress that when Texas joined the union, it passed a law saying the state could subdivide into four or five other states. Many Southerners liked this idea since it would permit more slavery-friendly Southern representation in the Senate. But Texans didn't take the bait. Their later frantic need for funds, however, forced politicians to sell a large chunk to the U.S. as part of the Compromise of 1850, which explains the state's right-angled western border.

Suppose Texas had retained all its original land? It would be twice its current size—over five hundred thousand square miles! That's a far cry from what Sam Houston described as "a spot of earth almost unknown to the geography of the age" in 1836.

Chapter II

To Serve God and Get Rich

"Over all the region we saw vast and beautiful plains that would make good pasture. I think the land would prove very productive if developed by civilized men." —Cabeza de Vaca

THE FIRST TEXANS

It's uncertain when exactly the first Texans arrived thousands of years ago. In 1953 the skull remains of "Midland Minnie" discovered in Midland County were dated to be ten thousand years old. So was the skeleton of an ancient woman found in the 1980s near Leander, in central Texas. Another discovery at Waco uncovered the remains of a man and child covered with stone tools, a bone needle, and seashell beads. These early inhabitants stalked animals such as bison and deer, used stone drills, axes, and knives, and grew crops. Some tribes later started to make pottery, used bows and arrows, and traveled with dog companions.

Who were these primitives? It's hard to say. Few cultural remains exist because people didn't pass on written records or leave many artifacts. We do know the early agricultural Caddos stayed in the northeast region and called it *Tejas* which means "friends" or "those who are friends." David La Vere says in *The Texas Indians*: "By 1500 a variety of distinct Indian cultures had developed in Texas. Some, such as those in East Texas and along the middle reaches of the Rio Grande, depended heavily on corn horticulture but supplemented it with hunting and gathering. Others along the Gulf Coast and in far south Texas were mainly hunters and gatherers. They used corn little, if at all, maybe growing small gardens when they could. Still, at the beginning of the sixteenth century, Indians lived in virtually every part of Texas."

EARLY SPANISH EXPLORATION

After Columbus landed at the Bahamas in 1492, the Spanish began to explore areas around the Gulf of Mexico in search of riches, glory, and lands to colonize. Even Columbus made several more trips to the new world seeking Asian trade routes. Ponce de León and Balboa came later. Then Cortéz conquered the Aztecs and renamed their capital Mexico City. Other *conquistadors* also sailed to New Spain, looking "to serve God and get rich," as one put it. They included Alonzo Alvarez de Pineda, who mapped the Gulf of Mexico from Florida to Vera Cruz. and Cabeza de Vaca and Vasquez de Coronado, who looked for the lost Seven Cities of Cibola but found Wichita Indian villages in Kansas instead of gold. After Hernando de Soto's death at the Mississippi River, Luis de Moscoso Alvarado also marched through Texas but nearly starved to death before floating down the Mississippi in boats caked with tar. (He was near Spindletop, which later spewed billions in oil.) The discouraging reports of these explorers led Spain to abandon Texas for awhile, although the Crown established a few settlements by the Rio Grande in New Mexico, as well as the mission Corpus Christi de las Isleta, near El Paso, the oldest settlement in Texas. By 1676, however, it's believed that explorers made their way into Texas from all directions—the Gulf, Florida, and New Mexico, followed by later expeditions in the west and north.

The early Spanish called this province "Texas" or "the New Kingdom of the Philippines." Where did the name come from? The Indians of east Texas used the word "*tejas*" or variant spellings which meant "allies" or "friends." Other scholars attribute the origin of the state's name to the Teyas tribe who lived near the canyon country of the Llano Estacado. The Spanish also called the first mission in the area San Francisco de los Tejas.

Indian tribes harassed Spanish explorers from the start and influenced the Crown's retreat from the wilds of Texas. They killed Pineda and many of his soldiers in 1520. Juan Bautista Chapa mentions in *Historia* an early trip into south Texas against an Indian tribe: "In the year 1665 there were many military actions and a continuation of the uprising of the Indians from the north. The Indians appeared in several bands and advanced not only to the roads but even to the Spanish settlements, including Saltillo … and other settlements in this province. The Indians would rob and do as much damage as they could." The Pueblos killed four hundred

Painting of Indians greeting LaSalle's party in 1636 by George Catlin

Spaniards in 1680 over religious issues. LaSalle also clashed with the Karankawas. In *Relación* Cabeza de Vaca told about tribes who buried boys alive and "cast away their daughters at birth; the dogs eat them. They say they do this because all the nations of the region are their enemies, with whom they war ceaselessly and that if they were to marry off their daughters the daughters would multiply their enemies until the latter overcame and enslaved them."

Another setback besides savage Indians faced the Spanish—French colonization in Texas. Explorer La Salle got permission from Louis XIV of France to open a colony at the mouth of the Mississippi River, the same region claimed by Spain, but landed at Matagorda Bay on the Texas coast instead. When his ship got wrecked on a reef, losing most of its provisions, he decided to establish a stockade called Fort St. Louis. After trouble with disease, Indians, and crops, La Salle made several exploratory trips and was killed by his own men. The Karankawa Indians, meanwhile, attacked and wiped out the fort. It wasn't until five years later in 1689 that the governor of Coahulia, Alonso de León, found the settlement's ruins along with several skeletons.

When de León returned to Mexico, he praised the land of the Caddo Indians whom he visited, urging an expedition to central Texas near the Guadalupe River. A Franciscan padre, Damián Massanet, who traveled with de León, also praised the fertile land, which resulted in approval from the Crown. Father Massanet and de León started several missions in east

Texas but failed because of disease, floods, food shortages, and problems with the Caddos. Livestock set free eventually became wild longhorn cattle and the mustang ponies Indians used to hunt and attack settlers. The once-flourishing Caddos suffered from epidemics, as did other native tribes who met Europeans. Only nomads such as the Comanches managed to escape devastation.

Around 1700, the governor of Louisiana sought trade with the Spanish. He sent Captain Luis Juchereau de St. Denis who built a French post at Natchitoches on the Red River and began to trade with natives. In a joint French-Spanish effort, St. Denis led an expedition into Texas to make contact with the Indians. The Spanish established a handful of missions near the French outpost and soon realized the need for a supply place between the Rio Grande and East Texas—which is how San Antonio got its start.

San Antonio de Béxar

In the early seventeenth century, a Spanish expedition headed for East Texas came upon a place considered the most beautiful in all New Spain. Indians called it Yanaguana. The Spaniards changed the name to San Antonio de Padua in honor of St. Anthony of Padua. Years passed. Then two Franciscans came across the same place and urged the Crown to build a mission as part of a chain stretching across the province. Each settlement would include a mission and fort (*presidio*) with soldiers to protect missionaries and entice Indians to work and become Christian converts. In ten years, Spanish colonists would arrive and create towns.

In the spring of 1718, a mission called San Antonio de Valero (the Alamo) began along San Pedro Creek in honor of the viceroy of New

The Alamo (San Antonio de Valero) is one of the most famous historic sites in the U.S.

Chapter II: To Serve God and Get Rich

The Spanish Governor's Palace. Founded in 1718 as the Military Presidio de Bejar, it once housed the presiding governor for the region know as Tejas. It included a ballroom, small chapel, fireplaces, and a courtyard.

Spain. The nearby *presidio* became known as San Antonio de Béxar. One friar called this settlement "the best site in the world, with good and abundant irrigation water, rich lands for pasture, plentiful building stones, and excellent timber." But factions squabbled. For example, a group of families from the Canary Islands built their own town called the Villa de San Fernando separate from other soldiers-settlers-friars, and set up the first civil government in Texas. It was located between San Pedro Creek and the San Antonio River, in a place now known as Main Plaza. These people not only quarreled among themselves but with everyone else, which led mission authorities to call them "a gang of lazy, ignorant interlopers." Eventually, however, they mingled with the rest of San Antonio because of intermarriage, the growing cattle trade, and fear of Indian attacks. The church at Villa de San Fernando opened in 1849. Its sanctuary and dome remain a part of the present San Fernando Cathedral built in 1873.

San Antonio became the hub of activity in Spanish Texas with a population of around three thousand. But it grew slowly. A friar described this outpost in the middle of nowhere as having "fifty-nine houses of stone and mud and seventy-nine of wood, but all poorly built, without any preconceived plan, so that the whole resembles more a poor village than a villa ... The streets are tortuous and filled with mud when it rains." Another French navy captain who traveled across Texas in 1767 also noted that "as many of the houses are in ruins, it is but weakly fortified, and has much occasion for a stronger garrison. It is besides much incumbered [sic] from without by several miserable villages, which give encouragement to the incursions of the enemy. The space too inclosed [sic] by the angle of the river is crowded by a multitude of huts, which are occupied by a number of emigrants from the Canary Isles." This was long before Alamo City became known as "the jewel of the Southwest."

THE FIVE MISSIONS

Franciscans came to Texas in the late seventeenth century to "civilize" the Indians and spread Christian teachings. They started around forty missions in East Texas, along the Rio Grande, and in the San Antonio area. The location, climate, and peaceful Coahuiltecan Indians around San Antonio on the San Antonio River not only encouraged settlement but also gave the Spanish a halfway station for launching further missionary work. The Indians dug canals, grew crops, and tended livestock. Although friars locked the laborers' doors at night, some still ran away and were punished with whips and stocks. As one priest put it, "There are Indians who are hungry, and they accept the faith through the enticement of food ... and there are those who ... require the weapons of Your Majesty to bring them into civil society." The problem? Many of these nomadic Indians had no desire to become "civilized" or Christian converts. So fewer and fewer came to the missions which resulted in the system's gradual decline—although those built at San Antonio remained the most successful.

The five old restored Spanish missions stretch for eight miles along the winding San Antonio River—unique in North America because of their placement in town settings. The first, Mission San Antonio de Valero, became known as "The Alamo." The remaining four include Mission Concepción, Mission San José, Mission San Juan, and Mission Espada.

Mission San Antonio de Valero—The Alamo
This remains the most famous mission in Texas and the U.S. Several million people a year visit the restoration in downtown San Antonio. First

established in 1718, the mission's location changed several times. Missionaries tried to educate and Christianize Indians but disease and desertions led to its abandonment in 1793. Ten years later, the Second Flying Company of San José y Santiago del Alamo de Parras occupied the mission as a barracks. The Alamo's name either derives from these soldiers or the Spanish word *Alamo* for nearby cotton wood trees. Mexican forces remained here until General Martin Perfecto de Cos surrendered to Texas rebels in 1835. The next year General Santa Anna attacked the mission, leaving all but a handful dead and the buildings in ruin. After the Texas Revolution, the U.S. government used the Alamo as a quartermaster depot to supply frontier forts, although Confederates occupied it during the Civil War. Disputes over ownership continued until the Daughters of the Republic of Texas served as custodians of this national historic landmark for many years.

Mission San José

The "Queen of the Missions of New Spain," named for the governor of Texas, opened two years after San Antonio de Valero. It remains a glorious testament to Spanish settlement in the Southwest before the U.S. fought the Revolutionary War. Its rose window, seventy-five-foot bell tower, and intricate carvings are the best example of Spanish colonial sculpture in the U.S. One priest praised: "The mission can justly be called the metropolis of all those in New Spain; not because of the antiquity of its origin, but for the beauty of its plan, the strength of its construction, the grace and beauty of its edifices, the abundance of its defenses: there being no other in all the line of the frontier which deserves even a comparison with San José." By 1890, however, the mission's dome had collapsed, the ornate cedar paneled door had been stolen, and the sculptures had been disfigured by tourists. Today, the mission is restored to its full glory.

Mission Concepción

Built of adobe and limestone, Mission Concepción looks much as it did two hundred years ago, although the compound no longer exists. Its architecture is a combination of Renaissance, Moorish, Gothic, Romanesque, and American Indian motifs. Here James Bowie and James W. Fannin fought the Battle of Concepción in 1835. The mission later served as a supply depot for the U.S. army during the Mexican War. The least restored of the five missions, it still remains a stunning sight to behold.

Mission San José (Queen of the Missions)

Mission San Juan

Like Mission Concepción and Mission Espada, this mission was originally founded in East Texas and then moved to the present location in 1731 when France pushed Spanish settlement further west. It flourished for awhile providing produce for the other missions and garrisons, and started to build a new stone church but it also declined over the years.

Mission Espada

This first mission in Texas (1690) moved to the San Antonio River in 1731. Its *acequia* (irrigation) system includes the oldest stone aqueduct in the country. Because successful farming depended on water, the early settlers built irrigation ditches along with dams and aqueducts that brought water from the San Antonio River to the farm fields.

THE SWORD AND THE CROSS

The Spanish missions prospered for several decades and attracted the Coahuiltecan Indians who needed constant supervision. By 1762 nearby ranches included 5,500 cattle, 450 saddle horses, 1,280 mares, and 15,200 sheep and goats. Yet in 1793, only a handful of the original missions remained. Many Indians either deserted or died of poor health and diseases such as smallpox and cholera. Settlers, soldiers, and clerics argued and filed suits against one another. Military support diminished. It was also difficult to attract new colonists.

Political and military affairs at the missions and scattered towns were under the jurisdiction of a viceroy who conferred with a *junta* (general council) on important issues and then sought royal approval in Spain. In 1776 a commandant general didn't exist—except for the *villa* of San Fernando de Béxar where landowners not only elected an *ayuntamiento* (council) but also an *alcade* (mayor and justice of the peace). Other small settlements in Spanish Texas included Goliad, Nacogdoches, and Adaes (the capital).

By 1824 all five missions along the San Antonio River were secularized. That's because after the Seven Years' War (French and Indian War), the French returned Louisiana to Spain, ending their threat to Spanish settlement and the need to fortify its boundaries. Spain also refused to change rooted values and traditions to meet New World needs, considering their faith and culture superior to all others, and believing they could attract Indians without trouble. This system, called "reducing," failed. The impractical plan to stretch missions from Laredo to the Sabine River ignored the vast Texas wilderness and the military's inability to tame it. Many soldiers lacked discipline and were resented by the friars. And unlike in Peru and Mexico, the Spanish couldn't subdue the main hostile Indian tribes—the Apaches and Comanches who harassed Texans for generations.

As early as 1720, the Apaches raided San Antonio of livestock and terrified farmers on the southern plains. Padres later pleaded for a stone church to serve as a fortress, but Spain continued to resist spending funds on this remote settlement, although inspectors liked the area's water supply and grazing lands. The viceroy even reduced soldiers at presidios to fewer than 150 as protectors of the province. This left San Antonio area missions stranded in the middle of nowhere, where Indians supplied with French guns and powder could attack without warning. As a result, these missions relocated on the San Antonio River near San Antonio de Valero in 1731. By 1772, the garrison at San Antonio pleaded with the Spanish governor of Texas to smoke the peace pipe with the Apaches. But the Crown just saw Texas as a remote wilderness filled with worthless land.

Indians also clashed with one another. The Apaches had been pushed from the north by the Comanches, from the east by the Wichitas, and from the south by the Spaniards. They eventually began to accept gifts and protection from the Spanish to protect them from enemy Comanches in the north. This led to the founding of several doomed missions. Mission San Sába north of San Antonio failed to attract any Apaches during its short existence. Then in 1758, two thousand hostile Comanches on horseback attacked, along with several other tribes, taking scalps, decapitating, and burning the mission. As the surviving priest reported: "I saw nothing but Indians on every hand … arrayed in the most horrible attire. Besides the paint on their faces, red and black, they were adorned with the pelts and tails of wild beasts, wrapped around them or hanging down from their heads, as well as deer horns. Some were disguised as various kinds of animals, and some wore feather headdresses." The next year Comanches again raided and killed more soldiers, stealing horses and pack mules. This caused a punitive force of five hundred mission Indians and untrained militia under Colonel Parilla to assault Comanche territory. After a battle on the Red River, the defeated Parilla returned to San Antonio and lost Spanish respect. These two bitter blows led the Spanish to abandon plans to build missions for the Indians and conquer the warlike Apaches and Comanches.

Frontier terror increased after the San Sábá massacre and the Parilla expedition. Apaches continued to murder and plunder, stealing horses, cows, and equipment. Travelers went through Mexico to get from San Antonio to Santa Fe. Ranchers and haciendas in northern Mexico from Sonora to

Coahuila and Durango got hit by Comanches during the full moon. Even soldiers balked at crossing the Apache-Comanche plains. Chases were futile because the braves rode fast, split into bands, and knew trackless routes to follow. The governor of Texas reported, "If they continue with the same steadfastness, the desolation of the province will be consequent, irremediable, and immediate." Pioneers refused to settle in Texas because the Spanish government couldn't promise protection against smugglers, outlaws, and Indian attacks. So this province of New Spain remained undeveloped with only 2,500 Hispanics by 1790.

In the late 1760s, a Spanish nobleman, the Marqués de Rubí, spent two years inspecting posts from the Gulf of California to Los Adaes in Texas. He called the fort at San Sabá "as barbarous as the enemy [Indians] who attack it." Rubí considered most of the forts in east Texas and the San Sabá region useless and advised they be closed because of graft, inefficiency, and failure to meet frontier needs. He recommended that only San Antonio and La Bahia remain, and that the capital be changed from Los Adaes to San Antonio, which happened in 1772. Rubí also called for the extermination of the Lipan Apaches who had caused so much turmoil in the Coahulia-Texas region. When the Spanish king ordered settlers in east Texas to move to San Antonio, they got permission from the viceroy to return home with the condition that they remain far away from the French holding, Natchitoches. The group eventually settled in Bucareli and then the old mission Nacogdoches, which replaced Los Adaes as the regional center.

As for the Marqués de Rubí? He didn't get very excited over Texas and wrote the king of Spain: "The country should be given back to Nature and the Indians."

The Filibusters

Once the French Revolution started in 1789, the Spanish focused on European events rather than the uprisings in New Spain until around 1803, when France sold Louisiana to the U.S. Border issues began to surface, and Mexico sought independence from royalist Spain. The Spanish devised a three-pronged defensive plan that included maintaining their land, increasing garrisons and colonies, and keeping Americans at bay. All these initiatives failed because of Mexico's new-found thirst for independence. Some Mexican insurgents, such as Father Hidalgo and Father Morelos, took advantage of the moment and revolted, but ended up defrocked and executed.

Other revolutionaries called "filibusters" followed Miguel y Costilla

Hidalgo and José Maria Morelos. In military language, a filibuster is someone who leads an expedition into a foreign country without authorization. The term derives from the Spanish word *filibustero* meaning pirate or buccaneer. Sir Francis Drake, who raided Spanish colonies in the West Indies, and the later William Walker, who tried to promote an insurrection in the Mexican states of Sonora and Baja California, are two notable examples. Filibusters also crossed into Texas from Mexico for political and personal gain—but failed in their efforts. Three such early attempts involved Philip Nolan, Bernardo de Lara Gutiérrez, and James Long.

Philip Nolan is called the first of the Southwestern filibusters. His expedition of 1797 sought wild mustangs, trade with Mexicans, and possibly gold mines until the Spanish grew suspicious and surrounded the fortification of Nolan's well-armed band, killing him at a campsite north of current-day Waco in 1800. Although some soldiers hid in a cave, they were caught and waited years for the king of Spain to decide their fate—one out of five hanged.

France's sale of Louisiana to the U.S. angered Spain, and war seemed imminent until both countries agreed to create "Neutral Ground" between the Sabine River and a small stream called the Arroyo Hondo. Between 1806 and 1819, this area became a no-man's land full of outlaws, riffraff, and murderers. Finally in 1819, Spain and the U.S. signed the Adams-Onís Treaty which placed the Sabine River as a dividing line and made the "Neutral Ground" part of U.S. territory. The Spanish also yielded Florida to the U.S. for five million dollars, and the U.S. agreed to abandon any future claims on Texas. But Luis de Onís, Spanish Minister in Washington, still doubted U.S. intentions: "The Americans at present think themselves superior to all the nations of Europe, and believe that their dominion is destined to extend now to the Isthmus of Panama and hereafter over all the regions of the new world." Other Mexican officials showed similar concern.

Another rebel, Bernardo de Lara Gutiérrez, wanted to free Mexico from the "ignominious yoke of Spain." He became Father Hidalgo's envoy to Washington, D.C., and the first Mexican diplomat to receive recognition from the U.S. government. He asked for aid and praised the benefits of trade between Mexico and the U.S., but didn't make much headway with Secretary of State James Monroe because of the boundary issue. Monroe, however, said he "deserved great credit for having opened communication between two nations hitherto separated."

The undaunted Gutiérrez joined forces with West Point-trained Augustus Magee to recruit volunteers to invade Texas. Their Republican

Army of the North captured Nacogdoches and La Bahia. When Magee routed a royalist force, it enabled Gutiérrez to enter San Antonio and draw up a constitution on April 6, 1813, which stated: "Governments are established for the good of communities of men and not for the benefit and aggrandizement of individuals. When these ends are perverted to a system of oppression, the people have a right to change them for a better." He also appointed himself "President Protector of the Provisional Government of the State of Texas." Anglo-Texans, however, faulted some of the constitution's articles, such as its support of the Catholic Church and its edict that Texas was joined to the Mexican Republic, which ended any chance of help from the U.S. Later on, Augustin de Iturbide praised Gutiérrez for his part in the Mexican revolution.

Because of political intrigues, Gutiérrez was replaced by José Alvarez de Toledo who suffered a humiliating defeat against Spanish militarist Arredondo at the battle of the Medina River in 1813, losing around a thousand men. Arredondo not only executed wounded soldiers but ravaged the Texas countryside, killing over three hundred at San Antonio alone.

In 1819 merchant James Long also planned to declare a sovereign republic in Texas. His force of around three hundred took Nacogdoches and sent emissaries to solicit the support of pirate Jean Lafitte without luck. A Mexican force wiped out the settlement and survivors fled down the Trinity River where they joined Long and returned to New Orleans to regroup, but met defeat again by Royalists. A soldier later shot Long in Mexico City. His expedition was the first to fly a flag with a single star using the red and white stripes later adopted by the Confederate states during the American Civil War.

By the end of the 18th century, most people had deserted Texas, which the Spanish governor called a place of "chaos and misery." Small Spanish settlements remained at Goliad and around crumbling San Antonio, the two key towns, and a spattering of other remote places. One prelate lamented: "The province has declined day to day so that even though we still call ourselves its masters we do not exercise dominion over a foot of land beyond San Antonio." Fierce Indians again controlled the sprawling land. Then two historic events happened. Mexico declared its independence from Spain in 1821. And, fifteen years later, Texas declared its independence from Mexico.

.

Chapter III

Come and Get It!

"Texas will be the richest state in our Union, without any exception."
—Thomas Jefferson

After nearly three hundred years of rule, Spain's legacy in Texas included the following when the U.S. bought Louisiana: San Antonio de Béxar with its five missions and villa of San Fernando, La Bahia (soon renamed Goliad), and Nacogdoches—about four thousand people, including soldiers. It also started Trinidad de Salcedo and San Marcos de Neve. (San Marcos was abandoned in 1808 after a flood and Indian raids, and Salcedo in 1813.) Besides the rebellions of Philip Nolan, Gutiérrez, and James Long, Spain had recently put down the uprisings of Hidalgo in 1811. What else could happen?

THE MEXICAN REVOLUTION OF 1821

In 1821, Colonel Augustin de Iturbide revolted against Spanish conservative rule in Mexico, marching into Mexico City. At first the frontier governors of Texas and New Mexico remained loyal to the Spanish Crown, and California's governor called Iturbide's grandiose plan "absurd" and "a dream." All three, however, soon accepted a peaceful revolution, sparing the country any further bloodshed. In addition, Russia sought California, the U.S. Texas, and beyond. Iturbide even made the mistake of crowning himself Emperor Augustin I in 1822 and served for less than a year. This wasn't a good time for old-world pretensions.

Many of Spain's problems arose from policies that favored the privileged, kept out strangers, and resisted any change of traditions. Commandant-general Nava ordered that "any foreigners, particularly Americans" should be detained. He also had written the governor of Texas in 1795: "Exercise care about the types of material in circulation, for by this manner our religion, liking, state, cult, vassalage, and security may be lost." The result of such fears was underdevelopment that planted the seeds of rebellion. Stephen Austin said that "not twenty souls of civilized inhabitants" lived between the Sabine River and San Antonio—around four hundred miles—and bands of Indians roamed everywhere. Yet Spanish contributions remain in Texas: the names of many towns, streams (and all but one major river), as well as land titles, can be traced to Spanish grants, detailed records by authorities, and the charming missions.

THE EMPRESARIO SYSTEM

In September of 1820, Spain decreed all its dominions open to outsiders, provided they obeyed the monarchy's laws and constitution. This resulted in the *empresario* (agent or contractor) system on the frontier province of Texas to create a buffer zone between Spain and the U.S. Connecticut Yankee Moses Austin applied for the first *empresario* grant from the Spanish. He had married into money gained through iron mining, succeeded in mining and smelting lead in southwestern Virginia and Missouri (upper Spanish Louisiana), but lost a fortune in heavy investments during the Panic of 1819. But he still held a Spanish passport. Austin figured that starting a colony in Texas might help recover lost riches—as much as $18,000—by charging fees for services and selling goods to settlers. However, Governor Martinez in San Antonio, ordered to keep Americans out of Texas, needed to approve the petition. As Austin's son Stephen later recalled: "My father after a fatiguing journey on horseback of more than eight hundred miles reached Béxar in November. His reception by the Governor was discouraging. Antonio Martinez, the governor of Texas, was a European Spaniard by birth, and had received rigid instructions from Arredondo, the military commander-general not to permit foreigners, particularly North Americans, to enter Texas. My father, at his first interview, received a peremptory order to leave the Province immediately." Fortunately, the persuasive Baron de Bastrop helped get the governor's approval in 1821 with the understanding that Austin settle three hundred hard-working Catholic families. The Spanish seemed happy with this arrangement because they weren't farmers at heart, and saw an opportunity to populate the province at a small cost. Settlers, however, would also have to deal with the barbarous Indians.

Austin never reached Texas because he died of pneumonia on June 10,

1821, after arranging everything. His wife wrote: "Tell dear Stephen that it is his dieing fathers last request to prosecute the enterprise he had commenced, that he had set his heart two [sic] much on it but for some wise purpose, god had prevented his traveling the rode he had planed out."

Austin's son, Stephen Fuller Austin (1793-1836), reluctantly accepted the *empresario* contract. He had attended college for two years, ran his father's store and lead business, then became a member of the Missouri territorial legislature. Land speculation followed in Arkansas where the territorial governor appointed him circuit judge of the first judicial district. While his father petitioned to the governor of San Antonio, Stephen lived in New Orleans, studying law and working on a newspaper.

Young Austin traveled to San Antonio, where Governor Martinez approved rights to his father's grant. Each settler received 640 acres. A husband and wife were also eligible for another 320 acres and an additional 80 acres for every slave. Settlers originally paid Austin twelve-and-a-half cents per acre for each settler—ten times less than the cost of public lands sold by the U.S. government after the Panic of 1819—but the fee was later reduced to a flat fifty dollars. Austin liked the climate, land, and locality, praising "grapes in immense quantities on low vines" and "very good, rolling prairie black soil, sufficiently timbered." He chose an area along the Brazos and Colorado Rivers for his colony and made San Felipe de Austin on the lower Brazos its capital. Newspaper ads placed around the country got responses. Wealthy planter Jared E. Groce came overland with over fifty wagons, thoroughbred horses, and ninety slaves. Others followed and became known as the Old Three Hundred, among them Robert McAlpin Williams, "Three-Legged Willie," and Jane Long, called "the Mother of Texas" by some. Over the years, Austin received a handful of contracts and brought around five thousand settlers. His secretary-partner, Samuel May Williams, also got land for services, but later became embroiled in a land speculation deal which created a rift between him and Austin.

Several other *empresarios* also received contracts through the new Imperial Colonization Law of April 14, 1823. Green Dewitt's contract called for four hundred families west of Austin near the Guadalupe River, where he founded Gonzales (named after the Texas governor). Martin de León, a rich Spanish rancher, settled southwest of Austin near the Guadalupe River and started the town of Victoria (named after the first president of the Republic of Mexico). He and Dewitt bickered because land sections overlapped.

Other *empresarios* wanted the land to sell or grade and make money instead of settle it. As a result, many failed to fulfill settlement contracts. A few *empresarios* caused trouble. Haden Edwards, for example, also received a colonization grant in Mexico City that included the settlement Nacogdoches near the old Neutral Ground. He found some squatters (Mexican, Anglo, and Cherokee Indians) and demanded they produce titles or pay for the property. Other settlers claimed grants from Spanish officials. His quarrelsome attitude led Mexican officials to cancel the contract. Haden and his brother, Benjamin, then declared the Republic of Fredonia, forging an agreement with the Cherokees to divide the state. The rebels occupied a stone house on which they flew a red and white flag which red, "Independence, Liberty, and Justice." Stephen Austin became concerned with possible negative reactions in Saltillo and called the small group "infatuated madness." The Fredonian Rebellion collapsed when Austin's militia joined Mexican troops. Insurgents fled across the Sabine into the U.S. and Haden's lands, broken into three grants, were given to David G. Burnet, Joseph Vehlein, and Lorenzo De Zavala, who in turn gave them to the Galveston Bay and Texas Land Company. This incident alarmed the Mexican government which feared the U.S. would take the land by force.

THE FATHER OF TEXAS

Stephen Austin, "The Father of Texas," faced many obstacles during the early years of colonization that tested his leadership skills. After the Mexican Revolution, officials refused to recognize his grant signed under Spanish rule. So he went to Mexico City where two groups controlled power: the church and the military. Although he called the capital of 150,000 "a magnificent one" with its architecturally imposing buildings, he also remarked that "a great proportion of [the population] are most miserably poor and wretched, beggars are more numerous than I ever saw in any place of my life." Austin followed political procedures and Emperor Iturbide finally signed the papers. But he soon resigned. Fortunately, during his year's stay in Mexico City, Austin had learned Spanish, gained respect, and cultivated contacts with influential men which led the acting president to approve the petition. Austin later wrote: "From the first day of my arrival on Mexican soil I bid an everlasting farewell to my native country and adopted this, and in doing so I determined to fulfill rigidly all the duties and obligations of a Mexican citizen."

Austin's patience paid off. The Mexican government not only increased the number of acres for married settlers, but Austin received 100,000 acres

CHAPTER III: Come and Get It!

Portrait of Stephen F. Austin, "The Father of Texas"

as founder of his colony. He received an *empresario* contract in which the "liberty, property, and civil rights" of settlers were guaranteed. On his return home, Austin drafted "A Plan of Federal Government" with Ramos Arizpe, similar to the Spanish Constitution of 1812 and the U.S. Constitution. When Arizpe wrote the *acta constitucional* in 1824, it included elements of this document, which brought him renown as the "Father of Mexican federalism."

In 1824, Mexico passed the National Colonization Law, declaring Coahuila and Texas one state with a capital at Coahuila, seven hundred miles away from Texas. This created troubles because most of the population lived in Coahuila, and legislators in its capital, Saltillo, controlled elections and the passing of laws. This angered Texans who wanted stronger representation in the government. (Only José Erasmo Seguín, who represented Texas, had opposed the joining of the two states.) This legislature chose the Nueces River instead of the Rio Grande as the dividing point between Coahuila and Texas. It also drew up a constitution and appointed an *ayuntamiento* (four-man council) to rule each of four municipalities in Texas: Béxar, Goliad, San Felipe de Austin, and Nacogdoches.

Austin's colony suffered many hardships. Crops failed because of a drought. Seed and supplies were hard to locate. Bandits and Indian raids scared settlers, which caused many to leave the colony. But around 1823 when Baron de Bastrop, land commissioner, began issuing land titles, other settlers as well as original ones returned. These people formed a militia that made peace with the Tonkawas and punished the Karankawas, founded San Felipe on the Brazos River, and even opened a newspaper as well as stores, grist mills, and a cotton gin. Austin devised a set of Civil and Criminal Regulations to keep order in the colony, trying to balance loyalty to Mexican law while serving the democratic needs of colonists. He regulated all the colony's affairs. Governor Martinez wrote him: "You will cause them [the colonists] to understand that until the government organizes the authority which is to govern them and administer justice, they must be governed by and be subordinate to you."

Mexico's unstable government worried about Anglo settlement in Texas. Would this lead to an eventual revolt? The Louisiana Purchase, the election to the U.S. presidency of Andrew Jackson who favored expansion, and the Fredonian Rebellion all heightened fears of a U.S. invasion. In 1827 the Mexican government sent influential intellectual Manual Mier y Terán on an exploratory expedition to Texas. He expressed concern over the possibility of rebellion, saying the settlers "carried their constitutions in their pockets." In Eastern Texas, Anglos chose the best land and outnumbered Mexicans ten to one because few migrated to the wilds of this state. The elitist Terán also resented *Tejanos* (Mexicans who lived in Texas), calling them lazy and uninterested in farming. Commission cartographer José Maria Sanchez agreed, saying these people were "ignorant not only of the customs of our great cities, but even of the occurrences of our Revolution." Hostile Indians also concerned the Commission. So there wasn't much to praise about Texas.

When Terán returned to Mexico, he recommended that garrisons be strengthened in the province, ports opened along the Texas coast, and that Mexican, Swiss, and German settlement be promoted. He disliked the commercial trade between Texas and the U.S. as well as with England and France. He knew that Texans such as Stephen Austin saw the enormous value of exporting cotton abroad instead of to Mexico. Terán said the U.S. assumed certain rights and urged the Mexican government to take immediate action. "The North Americans have conquered whatever territory adjoins them. In less than half a century, they have become masters of extensive colonies which formerly belonged to Spain and France, and of even more spacious territories from which have disappeared the former owners, the Indian tribes."

Terán and General Santa Anna became national heroes. But Mexico stood in a desperate state, defaulting on loans, and having to borrow at exorbitant rates from crooked private sources. Even Mexico City was a shadow of its past glory. Could Texas be saved? When Bustamante replaced Guerrero as president of Mexico, he implemented Terán's plan to save Texas through the Law of April 6, 1830, which banned further U.S. emigration but not settlers from Europe such as Irish Catholics. The reason for this ban? Terán knew Americans would spread their own culture and customs instead of Mexico's. The law also forbade slaves being bought into the state and passed a general passport law. Terán was appointed federal commissioner of colonization to enforce this legislation and find colonists. The prohibition of slavery, of course, enabled Mexico to kill two birds with one stone, since without slaves Southern planters wouldn't migrate.

Austin found loopholes in the decree, reasoning that it shouldn't affect those contracts already in force. Terán agreed and made exceptions for those going to the Austin and Dewitt colonies. He also approved Martin de Leon's colony because Mexicans received special privileges. In turn, Austin played down the new law's shortcomings and praised its benefits: military protection against Indians, increased coastal trade with foreigners, and relief from militia duty. Bu this time, around ten thousand Anglos had settled in the province who shared with *Tejano* ranchers the desire to shape their own future.

PRE-REVOLUTIONARY SCRAPES

In 1830 the Mexican government built a military garrison at Anahuac on the Texas Gulf Coast to collect custom duties as prescribed in the Law of April 6, 1830. Its commander, Juan Davis Bradburn, provoked colonists by using slaves to construct buildings, capturing runaway slaves for labor, and confiscating needed supplies. Austin called him "incompetent" and "half crazy." Bradburn also imprisoned Francisco Madero, land commissioner, and closed all other Texas ports. When he arrested William Barrett Travis (later hero of the Alamo), colonists organized a militia force and several ships to attack, but waited for a cannon from Brazoria. They adopted the Turtle Bay Resolutions, pledging their "lives and fortunes" in support of General Santa Anna against Bustamante, the president of Mexico. When the commander arrived from Nacogdoches, he removed Bradburn and Mexican troops from the post, avoiding further friction.

Meanwhile, Texans loaded the cannon at Brazoria on a ship and tried to sail past Fort Velasco where the commander, Ugartechea, refused passage. A bloody battle followed. Although Ugartechea claimed the fort

Painting called "Emigration to the Western Country," depicting 19th-century settlers coming to the Texas wilderness

could survive an attack of ten thousand, he surrendered and returned to Mexico. This battle became known as the first clash between Texan colonists and the Mexican army.

Another clash occurred at Nacogdoches after Commander Colonel Piedras returned from Anahuac. When he ordered all weapons surrendered, resistance flared from Anglos who demanded that Piedras repeal the order and declare his loyalty to Santa Anna. He refused and an assault followed. Piedras retreated toward San Antonio but surrendered after nearly fifty Mexicans died and troops turned against him.

By 1832, few Mexican troops remained in Texas except those stationed at Goliad and San Antonio. Mexico sent General José Antonio Mexía to Texas with a fleet of five ships and four hundred troops to restore order. Stephen Austin, returning from the state legislature at Saltillo, joined him on the journey, explaining that Texans still remained loyal to Mexico and supported the Constitution of 1824. Colonists at Brazoria saluted Mexía, threw a party on his behalf, and explained events, which helped his positive report when returning to Tampico.

Mexía, however, misread the critical need for Texas reform. A convention met in San Felipe with Stephen Austin as elected president to voice grievances against Mexico related to the Law of April 6, 1830. Delegates adopted resolutions that included acceptance of immigration from the U.S., separation from Coahuila, and lands for the building of schools. Mexican authorities at San Antonio ignored the reforms because delegates failed to follow proper procedure. A second convention followed in 1833 with William H. Wharton serving as president. Its petition included the repeal of the anti-immigration law and called for a state of Texas. This included a constitutional draft, similar to the Massachusetts constitution, drawn up by a committee chaired by state newcomer Sam Houston, former governor of Tennessee. They printed this constitution in a fifteen-page pamphlet called "Form of Government of the State of Texas, Made in General Convention, in the Town of San Felipe de Austin, in the Month of April, 1833."

Austin took the petition to Mexico City. The new president, General Santa Anna, had left liberal Vice President Farias to restore order and the Constitution of 1824 while he retired at his hacienda. Although Austin got off to a good start with Farias, the civil war and a cholera epidemic delayed action, which caused the diplomats to lock horns. Shortly afterwards in 1835, Santa Anna reassumed the presidency, retired Farias, and replaced the federalist government with a centralist one. He dissolved congress and scrapped the Constitution of 1824 which he had earlier supported. Dissent erupted in several states. When Zacatecas in Central Mexico rebelled, troops killed several thousand and sacked the capital.

Austin conferred with Santa Anna who agreed to make concessions that included permitting Anglo settlement. The legislature of Coahuila-Texas, also passed reforms that allowed English to become the state's official language, broadened its land law, and gave citizens trial by jury. Austin returned home, stopping at Saltillo where he was put under arrest and returned to Mexico City. Authorities had intercepted a letter written to Texans telling them to obey all laws, but if statehood was denied, get ready for war. Officials held Austin in the Prison of the Inquisition without trial. The confused leader wrote home: "All I can be accused of is, that I have labored arduously, faithfully, and perhaps at particular moments, pationately [sic], and with more impatience and irritation than I ought to have shewn [sic] to have Texas made a State of the Mexican Confederation separate from Coahuila." Attorneys finally got Austin released on bail, but he remained in the Mexican capital until July 1835, attending dinners, operas, and masquerades.

Conditions remained rough in Texas. People lived in log cabins with dirt floors. Clothes were threadbare and money scarce. During a dry spell in 1822, people ate wild horses to survive. When Ranger William A. A.

"Big Foot" Wallace first saw Texas, he wrote home: "Such a sight I never saw … The water is scarcely fit to drink and no timber scarcely worth naming … People kill each other here every day … I would not stay if all my relations were here and I beg of you never to come to Texas." Noah Smithwick also recalled in *The Evolution of a State*: "There was no poultry, no dairy, no garden, no books, or papers as nowadays—and, if there had been, many of them could not read—no schools, no churches—nothing to break the dull monotony of their lives, save an occasional wrangle among the children and dogs." One female settler mused that Texas was "a haven for men and dogs, but a hell for women and oxen." Yet it held enormous growth potential. When Juan N. Almonte inspected the province in 1834, he praised the ports, navigable rivers, fertile soil, climate, and variety of products. He called Texas "the most valuable possession of the republic." Yet even he cautioned: "The Anglo-American settlers are influenced by self-interest and not by patriotism."

Settlers kept arriving in Texas to seek new fortunes. The population reached around 25,000 Anglos and slaves and 5,000 to 6,000 *Tejanos* who tended to live in the older communities such as San Antonio, Goliad, and Nacogdoches. Anglo-Texans shipped around 7,000 bales of cotton valued at $315,000 to New Orleans by 1834. They also traded corn, timber, salted meats, and the skins of deer and bear. Austin praised the industrious and intelligent settlers, hoping to keep out criminals and frontiersmen, as well as end troubles with the Indians, so Texas could become stable and productive. Raiding parties not only stole livestock but killed settlers. Cruel Comanches, who tortured captives, remained the worst offenders. The Cherokees and Tonkawas, however, became guides and military allies to homesteaders against the Comanches and Wichitas.

Organized resistance continued to grow during Austin's two-year absence. Politicians broke into two factions: a "peace party" which favored negotiation and a "war party" which talked revolution. Most settlers wanted to farm and pledged loyalty to Mexico. When Santa Anna sent troops to enforce the customs office at Anahuac, William B. Travis led a group that forced the Anahuac post's surrender in June 1835, causing some communities to send letters of apology to General Cos, commandant of the Eastern Interior Provinces. Cos demanded that insurgents such as Lorenzo de Zavala and William B. Travis be turned over to a military tribunal—an order Texans rebuffed because in the U.S. one was tried by a jury of peers. Cos also planned to send more troops. A committee finally called for a third convention called the Consultation.

The Mexican government freed Austin in 1835. He returned to

Velasco, Texas, and approved the Consultation at Washington-on-the-Brazos. He now realized the futility of peaceful efforts but also saw the need for unity among Texans and obedience in the ranks. The Consultation elected Henry Smith as governor and Austin as commander-in-chief of the army, although he lacked experience in the field.

The surrender at Anahuac worried Ugartechea, Commandant of Texas, who ordered the return of a six-pound cannon at Gonzales (about seventy miles east of San Antonio on the Guadalupe River) loaned to the Dewitt colonists for fighting Indians. The colonists refused its surrender. When Mexican dragoons arrived, people had already removed canoes and the ferry-boat to the river's other side, which prevented its crossing. More excited volunteers arrived who put a "come and get it" white flag on the cannon, then attacked the Mexican camp, forcing its troops to withdraw. The revolution against Mexico had begun.

[March 1836]

TEXAS
FOREVER!!

The usurper of the South has failed in his efforts to enslave the freemen of Texas.

The wives and daughters of Texas will be saved from the brutality of Mexican soldiers.

Now is the time to emigrate to the Garden of America.

A free passage, and all found, is offered at New Orleans to all applicants. Every settler receives a location of

EIGHT HUNDRED ACRES OF LAND.

On the 23d of February, a force of 1000 Mexicans came in sight of San Antonio, and on the 25th Gen. St. Anna arrived at that place with 2500 more men, and demanded a surrender of the fort held by 150 Texians, and on the refusal, he attempted to storm the fort, twice, with his whole force, but was repelled with the loss of 500 men, and the Americans lost none. Many of his troops, the liberals of Zacatecas, are brought on to Texas in irons and are urged forward with the promise of the women and plunder of Texas.

The Texian forces were marching to relieve St. Antonio, March the 2d. The Government of Texas is supplied with plenty of arms, ammunition, provisions, &c. &c.

CHAPTER IV

Within the Sound of the Drum

The proper name for the people of Texas seems to be a matter of doubt or contrariety: some calling them Texians, while others speak or write Texans, Texonians, Texasians, Texicans. We believe that, both by the Mexican and American residents of the country, the name commonly used is Texians ... It may also be considered the euphonious abbreviation of Texasian. But Texonian and Texasite are absurd epithets."
—Telegraph and Texas Register (1835)

After the battle of Gonzales, General Cos wanted to arrest Travis, Zavala, and other rebels. He landed at Copano on the Gulf Coast, then occupied Goliad, and finally took San Antonio de Béxar. But the general left only a few soldiers to guard the fort at Goliad, which led to its loss when Texans attacked in October 1835. The spoils included several hundred muskets, cannons, and other military equipment as well as severing Mexican supply lines between Copano and General Cos in San Antonio.

After rapid victories at Gonzales and Goliad, Texans marched to San Antonio under Commander-in-Chief Stephen Austin, who had just returned from imprisonment in Mexico and now preached war. He felt Mexican politicians broke their promises to loyal Texans, and that Santa Anna wanted to replace the Federal Constitution of 1824 with a central government, depriving colonists of rights. This motley group of around four hundred of Austin's followers, many untrained and weaponless, wore everything from buckskin breeches and moccasins to broad-brimmed sombreros and coonskin caps. Sent ahead to secure a campsite, James Bowie and James W. Fannin tangled with Mexicans near the old limestone Concepción mission, down the river from Béxar. Although caught in an awkward position, they fought off several fierce attacks with rifles that could hit a target at two hundred yards. (Seventy yards was the range of Mexican rifles.) Their detachment managed to advance under cannon fire, using the war cry "the cannon and victory." Mexicans broke ranks and fled. The Texans gave chase, killing or wounding several dozen and losing only one soldier.

Austin arrived shortly after the fight and pressed to attack Béxar immediately, but both Bowie and Fannin wanted to wait for reinforcements. Another skirmish several days later boosted Austin's confidence even more when Texans took a fort on the Nueces River, again firing from behind trees and causing nearly thirty casualties. Such easy wins, of course, led to the wrong conclusion—Mexican soldiers were easily whipped. Most Anglo Texans at the time disliked Mexicans anyway because of ingrained Southern traditions. One veteran of the Texas Revolution recalled, "I thought I could shoot Mexicans as well as I could shoot Indians, or deer, or turkey, and so I rode away to war." Another called Mexicans "degraded and vile; unfortunate race of Spaniard, Indian and African, is so blended that the worst qualities of each predominate." And David G. Burnet, president of the Ad Interim government, blamed the revolution on the "utter dissimilarity of character between the two people, the Texians and the Mexicans. The first are principally Anglo-Americans; the other a mongrel race of degenerate Spaniards and Indians more depraved than they."

Because of winter's fast approach, it was decided to call off the siege of Béxar and let the army return to Gonzales. But after learning of the camp's disorganization from a deserter, the order was countermanded, and an attack was made on December 5. The battle lasted until December 10 when Cos flew up a flag and surrendered. Under duress he agreed to leave Texas and restore the federal Constitution of 1824—a promise later broken.

While brash Texans celebrated a string of rapid wins against Mexico, the convention called the Consultation met at San Felipe de Austin in November 1835 to form a government. Two factions argued their cases: the War Party wanted to declare independence from Mexico, and the Peace Party, under Sam Houston, wanted to restore the Constitution of 1824 and remain part of Mexico. The latter won. Delegates pledged loyalty to The Declaration of the People of Texas in a vague document that stated Santa Anna's actions had forced them to create "an independent government … But [they] will continue to remain faithful to the Mexican government, as long as that nation is governed by The Constitution [of 1824]." This wording reduced differences between the War and Peace parties and sought to keep needed Mexican liberals and *Tejanos* as allies.

Delegates chose Henry Smith as governor and James W. Robinson as lieutenant governor—both war hawks. Sam Houston, former governor of Tennessee and famous fighter of the Creek Indians, became commander-in-chief of the untrained army, many restless drifters who William Travis called a "mob." Stephen Austin and several others left on a mission to find funds and volunteers in the U.S.

The Consultation also created a General Council of delegates who bickered from the start and lacked a check and balance system. Lorenzo de Zavala, later vice president of the provisional government, asked how they could enforce public powers of the Consultation when "each citizen is a king like unto Adam?" De Zavala's admonition came true. When Henry Smith and the council differed over an expedition to take Matamoros in northern Mexico, Houston left for east Texas to negotiate a neutrality treaty with the Cherokee Indians. Without strong leadership or clear policies, conflicts continued between Smith and the council, resulting in his impeachment and appointment of James W. Robinson as head of state—an act which threw the government into chaos as it waited for a convention to meet in March 1836. This helped aggravate the later Alamo defeat because the Matamoros expedition stripped the fort of supplies and arms, and left few to defend its walls.

THE ALAMO—VICTORY OR DEATH

Mexican dictator Santa Anna, who called himself the Napoleon of the West, now led an army of around six thousand in a gripping operation to take Béxar and Goliad. Moving through the mountainous region of northern Mexico, troops first suffered from severe heat, and then a blinding blizzard. By the time they reached the Rio Grande, many soldiers had either died or deserted. Food and water supplies ran low (hundreds of camp followers also needed rations), so they lived off the land, stealing and marauding along the way to survive. Indian raids weakened troops who lacked doctors and medicine to combat epidemics and casualties. Money remained scarce because of Mexico's recent civil strife. Meanwhile, General Jose Urrea's men advanced towards Goliad, which controlled the Texas coastline, winning skirmishes along the way and gaining most of the laurels.

On February 23, Santa Anna finally reached Béxar, which surprised the defenders of the Alamo who had expected a later spring attack, although rumors and scout reports had been trickling in for weeks. They needed men, gunpowder, and supplies to hold the old mission built as a village compound to keep out hostile Indians. The settlement's population

Painting of the Alamo by Theodore Gentilz (1885) showing an aerial view during the siege

now hovered around two thousand and stood on one of the key routes through Texas because the San Antonio River ran through it. During Spanish control of the region, Béxar served as the governmental seat but lost this title after the federal Constitution of 1824 joined it to Coahuila.

Except for the tall roofless church, the Alamo's adobe and stone walls weren't built to handle a massive siege. Nearly forty years before, the structure had deteriorated so badly that the Spanish offered it at auction. Commander James Clinton Neill wrote in January that the garrison would "become an easy prey to the enemy, in case of attack" unless reinforcements arrived. Houston wanted to blow up the mission and abandon it, but Governor Smith of the provisional government refused. Most Mexican officers and several governors agreed with Houston about the Alamo, preferring to strike deeper within Texas territory instead of Béxar and Goliad, but Santa Anna sought a military victory, contrary to the advice of wiser generals.

After Alamo commander Neill left because of family issues, his replacements—Colonel James Bowie (who commanded volunteers) and William Travis (who commanded regulars)—argued until Bowie fell ill and Travis became sole commander of the mission. He strengthened the weak walls with dirt and timber, dug inside trenches, and moved dirt around—but the structure needed a thousand defenders instead of two hundred. He knew that the survival of his men would depend on receiving help. As he'd complained earlier: "Our affairs are gloomy indeed. The people are cold and indifferent—They are worn down & exhausted with the war, & in consequence of dissensions between contending & rival chieftains they have lost all confidence in their own gov't and officials." *Tejano* Juan Seguín, who sought a revolt against Santa Anna, carried a message through lines that Texans wouldn't surrender. (Seguín later fought at the Battle of San Jacinto and held several political posts.)

When Santa Anna finally arrived in Béxar with around 2,500 troops, he had a red flag flown from a church belfry, which meant "no quarter given." In defiance, the headstrong Travis fired a shot from the mission's largest eighteen-pounder cannon. When James Bowie tried to negotiate with a message in Spanish asking for terms, the angered Santa Anna offered "no guarantees to traitors."

Shortly afterwards, as Mexican batteries began arriving, Travis wrote his famous message on February 24 which a courier got through Mexican lines to the press:

> *To the People of Texas & all Americans in the world—Fellow Citizens & Compatriots—I am besieged by a thousand or more of the Mexicans under Santa Anna. I have sustained a continual Bombardment & cannonade for 24 hours & have not lost a man. The enemy has demanded a surrender at Discretion, otherwise, the garrison are to be put to the sword, if the fort is taken. I have answered the demand with a cannon shot, & our flag still waves proudly from the walls. I shall never surrender or retreat. Then, I call on you in the name of liberty, of patriotism & every thing dear to the American character, to come to our aid, with all dispatch. The enemy is receiving reinforcements daily & will no doubt increase to three or four thousand in four or five days. If this call is neglected, I am determined to sustain myself as long as possible & die like a soldier who never forgets what is due to his own honor & that of his country. VICTORY OR DEATH William Barret Travis*

Few farmers rallied to the cause. A small relief column from Gonzales managed to evade Mexican soldiers and enter the Alamo. Travis even wrote to the delegates at Washington-on-the-Brazos, who were forging a new constitution. He also sent several messages to Fannin at Goliad who started out in late February, but when several wagons broke down after half a mile, and oxen couldn't pull artillery across the swollen San Antonio River, he returned to reinforce Goliad against an assault from General Urrea. Sam Houston complicated matters by refusing to believe reports of Mexican soldiers in Béxar. It must be remembered that most rebels arrived after the rebellion started. One politician called them "violent and desperate men who have nothing to lose."

An engraving showing the Mexicans storming the Alamo

The Alamo battle lasted for thirteen days. For twelve days, both sides exchanged sporadic fire. Mexican cannon damaged the mission's walls and wooden supports while defender rifles picked off soldiers who exposed themselves. While waiting for reinforcements, Santa Anna sent out patrols to intercept troops of Fannin or Houston, digging entrenchments each night to get within shooting range. He also taunted those inside the Alamo with music, bombardments, and loud noises—anything to erode confidence. Defenders snuck out at night and burned houses that gave protection to the enemy and collected wood and foodstuffs.

Santa Anna finally decided to attack and called a meeting of senior officers. Some preferred to wait for bigger cannons or just starve out the traitors in a few weeks. They also worried about the wounded without surgeons or field hospitals. Was taking the Alamo worth so much bloodshed? But Santa Anna still ordered an assault early the next morning after a cold front had left his men damp and chilled.

Alamo legend says Travis drew a line with his sword and asked those who wanted to fight and die to step forward. Only one person stayed behind the line. Even the ailing Bowie supposedly had his cot carried across the line. Where fact ends and fable begins at this historic battle will always remain blurred. Time had run out. Command knew they'd lose the old mission without help—but chose to stay and fight because they still expected last-minute reserves. Besides, the General Council had insisted that under no conditions should they "abandon or surrender the place" unless in the "last extremity." The Alamo must be saved because of its strategic location.

Chapter IV: Within the Sound of the Drum

An engraving showing the fighting at the Alamo after Santa Anna's army breached its walls

On Sunday, March 6, 1836, Santa Anna's forces attacked before dawn to the bugle cry of the "*deguello*," a verb that meant "to slit the throat." Hearing the alarm, Travis supposedly shouted: "Come on, men! The Mexicans are upon us and we'll give them hell!" Cannons spewed fire. Rifles cracked. Battle cries filled the frosty air. Less than two hundred men faced over two thousand.

Mexican troops circled the Alamo and attacked with crowbars, axes, spikes, and scaling ladders. Travis was one of the first to die with a musketball through the head. Confusion and carnage followed. Although the rebels fought off several attacks, wave after wave of Mexican soldiers breached the walls, battered down doors and windows, and gained control of the mission's cannon. Many Mexican soldiers were trampled to death by their own frenzied comrades. One aide reported, "It seemed as if the furies had descended upon us." He remembered: "The sharp retorts of the rifles, the whistling of bullets, the groans of the wounded, the cursing of the men, the sighs and anguished cries of the dying, the arrogant harangues of the officers, the noise of the instruments of war, and the inordinate shouts of the attackers who climbed vigorously bewildered all ... The shouting of those being attacked was no less loud and from the beginning had pierced our ears with desperate, terrible cries of alarm in a language we did not understand."

Unable to survive such formidable odds, defenders fought from room to room, in the courtyard and barracks, finally making a last stand in the church. Bowie died in one of the barrack rooms. Most believe folk hero Davy Crockett was also killed. Mounted lances cut down those who fled over the walls. One fighter later wrote: "The scene was one of such horror

Davy Crockett, 1839

Chapter IV: Within the Sound of the Drum

Painting by Louis Eyth (1870) depicting the death of Bowie at the Alamo

that it could never be forgotten by any one who witnessed its incidents." The battle left around eight hundred dead—including everyone in the Alamo except for a few. Santa Anna considered the fight a small affair, but his generals fumed. U.S. newspapers called Santa Anna everything from a "tyrant" to a "butcher" and "bloody tiger." The *New York Post* accused: "Had he treated the vanquished with moderation and generosity it would have been difficult if not impossible to awaken that general sympathy for the people of Texas which now impels so many adventurous and ardent spirits to throng to the aid of their brethren." Cities raised thousands of dollars—and Jackson's government in Washington finally took notice. Both the U.S. and Mexico now recognized the enormous future agricultural potential of Texas.

THE CONVENTION OF 1836

While Santa Anna's forces were battering the Alamo, the Convention of 1836 was meeting at Washington-on-the-Brazos during rainy weather in "an unfinished house, without doors or windows." Cotton cloth stretched over openings only partially kept out the "cold wind." The Convention's intent? To found a Republic of Texas separate from Mexico and to create a constitution. Only two of the fifty-nine delegates were native

Texans. George C. Childress from Tennessee chaired the committee and wrote most of the document patterned after the American Declaration of Independence. Unanimously approved on March 2, it declared Texas a free and independent republic.

The Convention then drafted a Constitution modeled after that of the U.S. but diverging in its restriction of power. People could hold slaves but could not import them from outside the states, although future settlers could bring slaves with them. Free slaves needed congressional approval to remain in Texas. Its ad interim government chose David G. Burnet as president, Lorenzo de Zavala as vice president, and Sam Houston as commander-in-chief of all land forces of the Texas army, both regulars, volunteers, and militia. Those who died at the Alamo never knew that Texas had politically declared itself a republic.

Soon after the Convention adjourned, President Burnet removed all state papers to Harrisburg and then Galveston because thousands of Mexican soldiers had crossed the Rio Grande. Houston retreated to Gonzales, deciding to use guerilla tactics instead of fighting from forts, but must have wondered how he could win with such an unruly bunch of brawlers.

MASSACRE AT GOLIAD

Santa Anna made the mistake of waiting after defeating the Alamo, thinking the Texas rebellion had ended, but Mexico's General Urrea moved quickly up the Gulf coast, crushing the Matamoros Expedition led by Frank Johnson and James Grant. This offense had sought to cripple the Mexican government and gain support of federalists in Mexico who opposed Santa Anna. It also offered Johnson an opportunity to plunder and Grant to regain lost land. Houston insisted Texas should declare statehood instead of invading Mexico. Many volunteers changed their mind, but Johnson and Grant still left for San Patricio to find horses. The governor also authorized James F. Fannin to embark on such a mission, but he chose to stay at La Bahia, the fort at Goliad, and renamed it Defiance.

Local *Tejanos* kept Urrea informed of insurgent movements. As a result, the general surprised Johnson at San Patricio during a cold, rainy night in late February, killing all except Johnson and several others. Urrea then set a trap for Grant near Agua Dulce Creek, leaving him and forty others dead on the field. One man escaped and warned Fannin, who remained convinced they could handle an attack. As one surgeon wrote: "Prepared as we were we fully believed ourselves able to make a stand against many times our numbers, not doubting but that on being attacked, the citizens

La Bahia (Goliad). Originally built by the Spanish in 1749 to protect nearby missions, this is a 1960s reconstruction of the presidio that played a major role in the fight for Texas independence.

would at once come to our support and enable us to maintain the fort, or failing in that to fall back upon some other position and continue the resistance until it should ultimately be successful." But again, old settlers failed to show. Instead troops from the U.S. arrived: the Red Rovers, the Mustangs of Kentucky, the New Orleans Grays, the Mobile Grays, and others, all anxious to fight Mexicans.

When Houston learned of the Alamo defeat, he sent Fannin a letter from Gonzalez, saying to retreat to Victoria as soon as possible and sink what artillery couldn't be taken. He also told Fannin to blow up Goliad. But Fannin had dispatched a force with carts and teams to help stranded families at Refugio nearly thirty miles away. The fall of the Alamo and Houston's retreat led terrified colonists to flee the area—which became known as the Runaway Scrape. Even the provisional government bolted from Washington-on-the-Brazos to Harrisburg. As one Texan recalled: "The desolation of the country through which we passed beggars description. Houses were standing open, the beds unmade, the breakfast things still on the tables, pans of milk moulding in the dairies ... There were

A pen-and-ink drawing by Norman Price of the massacre of Fannin's troops

broken-down wagons and household goods scattered all along the road." Advanced troops of General Urrea, however, cornered this Refugio force in the mission where a fight ensued, resulting in a need for reinforcements. Fannin sent a relief force which weakened Fort Defiance's defenses.

Each day Fannin waited for the return of both detachments, unaware of General Urrea's position. A courier finally brought news of the defeat. Then in mid-March, instead of leaving for Victoria, a skirmish between some of the garrison's men and Mexican rancheros ensued. This cost Fannin precious time. A thick fog gave cover the next morning as the garrison finally retreated to Victoria with heavy baggage and artillery, torching the fort, and creeping along because of stubborn oxen. A cart broke down while crossing the San Antonio River, forcing them to fish a cannon from the water. Then stubborn oxen decided to graze. When Fannin finally reached an area of low ground about a mile from timber, another broken cart required the transfer of baggage and ammunition. That's when enemy cavalry appeared and shooting started.

The Battle of Coleto—ten miles from Goliad and fifteen miles from Victoria—lasted from early afternoon until dusk. Instead of retreating to the shelter of woods about a mile away, Fannin placed the column into a hollow box formation with cannons on each side and fought off repeated assaults by General Urrea's forces. Although the Texans were remarkable marksmen, their location in an open field of high grass on a lower level than the enemy without access to water weakened the group's position. Fighting was savage. Horses kicked off riders and trampled them in the dust. "They came in full tilt, with gleaming lances, shouting like Indians," explained a Texan officer. A witness later reported: "The scene was now dreadful to behold; killed and maimed men and horses were strewn over the plain, the wounded were rending the air with their distressing moans, while a great number of horses without riders were rushing to and from back upon the enemy's lines, increasing the confusion among them."

Although well supplied with guns and cannon, ammunition soon ran low, and cannons overheated without water to sponge them. Night fell. The Mexicans withdrew instead of storming the camp. Fires couldn't be lit because enemy sharpshooters would pick off men. "The cries of pain uttered by the stricken soldiers, the muffled thuds arising from the buildings of our barricades, and the challenges of the Mexican sentries broke the silence in the prairie, which lay dark and cheerless around us. There was not the smallest breath of air, and the moisture of the atmosphere added to the discomfort of our wounded companions."

Fannin refused to retreat under cover of darkness and leave the wounded behind, knowing the fate of prisoners at the Alamo as well as Johnson and King's men. Instead, he dug ditches and placed carts, corpses, and dead animals around camp wagons for the next day's fighting. By early morning, Urrea's army had swollen to between seven hundred and one thousand men. Fannin flew a white flag and a ceasefire followed during which his men surrendered under the presumption they would be treated as prisoners of war, given medical care, and eventually freed. Although Urrea sought clemency for the Goliad survivors, Santa Anna issued an execution order. On Palm Sunday, Mexican soldiers killed around 350 men, including James W. Fannin, who was shot in the face and thrown in a ditch.

Santa Anna had now outraged Mexican and U.S. diplomats once again. The Goliad massacre, along with the Alamo defeat, led some Texas colonists to finally rise against the despotic government of Mexico. General Urrea wrote that he "never thought that the horrible spectacle of that massacre could take place in cold blood and without immediate urgency, a deed proscribed by the laws of war and condemned by the civilization of our country."

Portrait of Sam Houston by S. Seymour Thomas

CHAPTER IV: Within the Sound of the Drum   49

Engraving of the Battle of San Jacinto

EIGHTEEN MINUTES AT SAN JACINTO

Learning that the Texas government had moved from Washington-on-the-Brazos to Harrisburg, Santa Anna made a tactical error and decided to capture its leaders instead of finding Sam Houston's rag-tag army—a decision that left Mexican troops exposed to a hostile wilderness. The death of the acting president of Mexico, a loyalist, may have prompted this decision, so Santa Anna could quickly return to Mexico. Perhaps he wanted to upstage General Urrea's triumphs in the field.

Houston, meanwhile, left Gonzales and retreated eastward toward the U.S. border after learning about the Alamo and Goliad disasters. By the time he reached the Colorado River, his troops included around 1,400 men, although desertions continued. Then he moved through swamps and bogs to Groce's Crossing on the Brazos River where two cannons (the Twin Sisters) arrived as a gift from Cincinnati to replace those lost at Gonzales. The restless men grew mutinous as rain turned roads and trails to mud. But Houston kept on the move without supplies, articles of war, or support from the government, sending out scouts to keep track of Santa

Santa Anna, General/President of Mexico, 1847

Anna's whereabouts. Scouts somehow intercepted several couriers whose saddlebags included dispatches from Santa Anna that showed he was "within the sound of the drum," and that General Cos would soon arrive with more soldiers.

Houston grabbed the moment and gathered troops around him, shouting: "The army will cross [Buffalo Bayou] and we will meet the enemy! Some of us may be killed and must be killed, but soldiers remember the Alamo! The Alamo!" Troops also began to chant: "Remember the Alamo! Remember Goliad!" One lieutenant remarked: "After such a speech, but damned few will be taken prisoners—that I know."

Houston dug in around a dense grove of moss-covered oak trees near the Harrisburg Road where Buffalo Bayou met the San Jacinto River. An open field about three-quarters of a mile long separated this force from Santa Anna's campsite with a marsh behind it and a part of San Jacinto Bay on the right flank, which suited frontier riflemen but hindered the Mexican cavalry. One recruit later wrote: "Around 10 or 30 campfires stood as many groups of men: English, Irish, Scots, Mexicans, French, Germans Italians, Poles, Yankees, all unwashed and unshaven, their long hair and beards and mustaches matted, their clothes in tatters and plastered with mud. A more savage looking band could scarcely have been assembled."

Houston finally allowed an officer to reconnoiter, but not engage the enemy—an ignored order that nearly cost the death or capture of secretary of war Thomas Jefferson Rusk. Others joined the skirmish and managed to repel the enemy with only a few casualties before night fell. This reckless act angered Houston, but most of the troops now wanted to fight without his consent. The next morning General Cos arrived with around five hundred troops, leading volunteers to destroy a nearby bridge so more Mexicans couldn't get through. Houston and most officers wanted to wait for Santa Anna's attack, but relented to the army's frantic desire for action. Around four o'clock on April 21, 1836, he gave the word to march. For some strange reason, Santa Anna had failed to post guards. Many soldiers had fallen asleep during siesta time. Others were busy cooking, eating, or repairing equipment. The rebels got within two hundred yards before being sighted. Some soldiers stood and fought, but most fled for their lives as cannons and small-arms smoke shrouded the field.

The battle lasted around eighteen minutes. As one officer remarked: "Every man was his own captain, fighting his own way with only one aim—to kill Mexicans. Orders given to commanding officers were drowned in the noise or little heeded. In fact little semblance of order existed after the fight began. It seemed that every fighter was transformed into a wild, furious beast with but one impulse, and that to slay." Two of Sam Houston's horses fell from wounds, and the tobacco-chewing leader suffered a painful ankle wound. When the clash ended several hours later, 630 Mexican soldiers had been killed and 730 captured, while only 9 Texans died and 30 were wounded in the clash. After the slaughter, Houston made the oft-quoted remark: "Gentlemen! I applaud your bravery. But damn your manners!"

During the melee, Santa Anna managed to escape and hide in high grass near the bayou, where scouts found him wearing the shabby clothes of a slave with a linen shirt and diamond studs still underneath. When he was brought into the Texas camp, Mexican troops cried out, "El Presidente, El Presidente." This exposed his identity. Many Texans demanded, "Shoot him, hang him!" Instead Houston forced Santa Anna to compose a document stating the Mexican army would leave Texas, and the Rio Grande would become the boundary line between Mexico and The Republic of Texas. (Santa Anna would later ignore this document, saying it represented his wishes, not those of Mexico.)

The retreating Mexican army got bogged down in a sea of mud and muck because of a torrential storm, abandoning much of their gear and becoming more concerned about survival than a fight. This natural disaster sabotaged any plans on the part of generals to continue an immediate war with Texas. Besides, the Mexican government lacked resources to launch a second major campaign, either from Goliad or Matamoros. Times were also changing. The exploding U.S. population, fueled by cheap slave labor, would lead more Anglos to settle in Texas.

Although barely mentioned in histories, San Jacinto remains one of the most important battles ever fought in American history. It led to the Mexican War, which resulted in the U.S. acquisition of Texas and around a million square miles of new territory including Nevada, Arizona, Utah, California, New Mexico, and parts of Wyoming, Colorado, Kansas, and Oklahoma.

Chapter V

A Rich Jewel Lying Derelict

"Independence is the prize for which we battle."
—Sam Houston

Following the battle of San Jacinto, ad interim President David G. Burnet and General Santa Anna signed the Treaty of Velasco. This agreement stated Mexico would withdraw to south of the Rio Grande, pay for damages to private property, free Texas prisoners of war, and that Santa Anna would try to get the Republic of Texas recognized by the Mexican government. Houston, meanwhile, sailed for New Orleans to get a wound treated, and Secretary of War Rusk became military commander. The Mexican government, of course, refused to honor Santa Anna's treaty, and the dictator temporarily withdrew from politics.

Burnet's government faced many dilemmas. The volunteer army defied discipline, some rebellious officers planned a coup that included an invasion of Mexico, and the treasury coffers were empty. Few crops and scattered livestock meant hard times ahead for farmers. Indian raids and the possibility of another Mexican clash terrified settlers. Some Texans wanted to lynch Burnet—especially for letting Santa Anna go free. As conditions worsened, he called for an election in September to ratify the Constitution, decide on the annexation issue, and elect officials and the first president of the new struggling Republic.

THE RAVEN BECOMES PRESIDENT

Political parties didn't exist in Texas, so the republic's first election became a popularity contest. Candidates included Henry Smith, head of the provisional government, Stephen F. Austin, and Sam Houston, who entered the race at the last minute. Because of the victory at San Jacinto, he received nearly 80 percent of the votes. His political rival Mirabeau B. Lamar became vice president. Voters also approved the Constitution and annexation to the U.S. Houston then appointed Austin as secretary of state, Smith as secretary of the treasury, and Rusk as secretary of war. James Pinkney Henderson, later the first governor of Texas, served as attorney general.

During his two-year administration, Houston tried to keep peace with Mexico and the Indians, especially the Cherokees who had given him the adopted name Raven. When Comanches and Kiowa Indians continued to raid frontier settlements, Congress formed a corps that later became the Texas Rangers. Houston also managed to solve the brittle army problem by giving most troops a vacation, then not calling them back into service. Because the republic lacked a tax system, money remained so scarce the secretary of the treasury lacked funds to even buy stationery. So the government issued $650,000 in promissory notes which held their value for awhile, but then dropped to 65 cents on the dollar because there wasn't anything to back them up.

Houston made few reforms as first president of the Republic of Texas, partly due to the Panic of 1837 which crippled the U.S. and the ability of speculators to buy Texas bonds and lands. Both France and England also feared that support of the new republic would jeopardize their trade and investments with Mexico. One minister to Mexico said that stopping funds would "derange the whole monetary system of England." Texas's financial debts continued to rise because of meager income from taxes and tariffs. Houston wasn't eligible to run for a second term. (The Constitution limited the first president's term to two years instead of three.) Vice President Mirabeau B. Lamar won the 1838 election, and David G. Burnet became the new vice president.

MIRABEAU B. LAMAR: POET PRESIDENT

The political views of Lamar and Houston clashed. In his first message to Congress, former newspaperman Lamar threatened: "If peace can only be obtained by the sword, let the sword do its work." He wanted to expand Texas instead of joining the U.S. Union (an idea that irked many people), and to dispose of Indians and educate the public—all issues Houston opposed. But Lamar drove the Republic heavily into debt and caused more trouble for both Mexico and hostile Indians.

Foreign Affairs

During the Lamar administration, several powerful foreign countries recognized the Republic of Texas. France signed a commercial treaty in 1839 and even built an embassy in Austin. By the end of 1840, the Netherlands, Belgium, and England also made treaties with Texas, the latter hoping to annex it as part of the British Empire. To this end, England and Texas signed three separate treaties. The first promised commerce and friendship, the second agreed to let England act as negotiator between Mexico and Texas, and the third tried to reduce the slave trade by allowing searches of Texas ships, a provision Texans resented.

When diplomacy with Mexico proved futile, Lamar offered to support a revolt in the Mexican state of Yucatan that failed because the state made peace with Mexico. Then several hundred Texans joined Mexican insurgents, trying to create a republic in northern Mexico called the Republic of the Rio Grande, and fought several battles along the Rio Grande, although the Republic of Texas remained officially neutral.

Lamar's biggest blunder was the Santa Fe Expedition. Expansionist Lamar remained cool to the annexation of Texas with the U.S.: "I cannot regard the annexation of Texas to the American Union in any other light than as the grave of all her hopes of happiness and greatness." His dream of making the Republic of Texas a "great empire" that would spread from the Gulf of Mexico to the Pacific Ocean included opening business ties with Santa Fe which sat within Texas boundaries and promising riches to those who controlled it. But this grandiose plan to persuade those who lived in Santa Fe to cut all ties with Mexico and formally join Texas backfired. When the U.S. Congress refused to finance such a "wild goose campaign," as U.S. President Andrew Jackson later called it, Lamar still dispatched a caravan of three hundred men, thinking New Mexico would welcome Texans with open arms. Lamar wasn't the first politician to see the commercial value of the Santa Fe trail, which linked the Southwest with St. Louis. Stephen Austin also considered such a plan. Albert Sidney Johnson, secretary of war, likewise wanted to build a road from Austin to Santa Fe, and even Houston liked the idea of spreading to the West. A journalist who went with Lamar's expedition remembered that "as for having anything like a regular battle, or forcibly subduing the country should the inhabitants be found hostile, such events were neither intended nor talked of. Invading armies, when hard fighting is anticipated, seldom take merchandise with them to sell to their enemies."

These pioneers left Austin for Santa Fe in June 1841 without trusted guides and late in the season to avoid the summer drought—unaware

Engraving of the Battle of Plum Creek

their destination remained about 1,300 miles away. They suffered from heat, shortages of food and water, prairie fires, stampedes, and Comanche Indian attacks. After more than three months, they finally reached the town, whereupon Mexican militia arrested everyone and marched them off to Mexico City, two thousand miles away. Some were shot and others treated harshly. Survivors spent long months chained, crammed together, and imprisoned with lepers while U.S. and European diplomats tried to free them. Thus expansionist efforts got off to a slow start.

INDIAN AFFAIRS

By the start of Lamar's administration, the Cherokee and other Indian tribes in eastern Texas tired of waiting for treaties that promised rights to hunting grounds. Raids resulted. When Texans found papers on a marauding party that implicated the Cherokees in an Indian-Mexico alliance to invade Texas, Lamar accused them of "treasonable correspondence" and of giving "countenance" to the Mexican government. Negotiations broke down and the army killed one hundred Cherokee warriors at the Battle of the Neches, herding others across the Red River into Oklahoma's Indian territory.

The hostile Comanches not only continued to kill and torture settlers, but after beating the army in several clashes, asked for a peace meeting. The Council House Fight in San Antonio ensued. Although Texans told the Comanches to bring in all white captives, they arrived with only one abused, mutilated girl. In an attempt to take chiefs as hostages, troops killed a dozen chiefs and numerous warriors. Five hundred Comanches under Chief Buffalo Hump took revenge. They attacked Victoria and sacked Linnville, near Port Lavaca, killing captives. Texans trailed and defeated the Comanches at Plum Creek and on the upper Colorado River, crushing their forces, although scattered raids continued. This Texan victory achieved two important ends: The Comanches left central Texas

Engraving of the first capital building in Texas

which helped frontier settlement; it also stopped Mexico's plan to recruit Indians for another assault on Texas.

THE CAPITAL

The capital's location continued to cause conflict between Lamar and Houston. Neither wanted the temporary Columbia location. Houston relocated it in 1836 to a two-story frame building in the village of Houston. Then Lamar chose a hamlet between the Trinity and Colorado River called Waterloo, a site removed from settlements and open to Mexican and Indian raids. Congress changed the hamlet's name to Austin after Stephen F. Austin who had recently died of pneumonia. In 1839, the government moved in with forty wagons full of furniture and documents—but not for long. In 1842, with the fear of Mexican troops on everyone's mind, the capital again changed to Washington-on-the-Brazos, although many papers remained in Austin, which permanently became the capital after annexation in 1846.

HOMESTEAD AND EDUCATION ACTS

Lamar's two most progressive policies were the 1839 Homestead Act and the Education Act. The former enabled a homeowner sued by creditors to keep his home, furniture, and tools. The latter provided for future education in Texas. It set aside around fifteen thousand acres for each county to provide a public academy and another quarter of a million acres for two universities. Although education remained on the back burner because of funds, several private academies and colleges, including Baylor University and Southwestern University, opened during the Republic. Later the free school system and University of Texas would result because of this foresight.

Unfortunately, Lamar's extravagant army and Indian programs strapped the Republic, raising its debt from two to seven million dollars. He secured only one loan from the Bank of the United States and failed in creating a government-owned Texas bank. When he left office, the value of "red backs" (notes) had fallen to around 15 cents on the dollar. The Republic remained penniless, even with recognition from European powers and offering land grants to colonists.

THE RAVEN RETURNS

Houston used every excuse to demean Lamar, both privately and publicly. He lamented: "Oh my country! No one can fancy its affliction, and every day only adds to its calamities … No patriot can anticipate the future prospects of Texas without the most acute, and heavy anguish." In 1841 he again ran for president against David G. Burnet, vice president under Lamar, and won by a two-to-one margin on a ticket that promised cutbacks. "We are not only without money, but without credit, and, for want of punctuality, without character, " he rebuked Congress. Houston reduced salaries, limited the circulation of paper money, and downsized the army and Texas Rangers. Peace policies with the Indians also received top priority. He met with Comanche Chief Buffalo Hump and signed a treaty to open a chain of trading houses on the frontier to help keep peace and provide revenues. Yet debts still reached around twelve million dollars.

How could a republic with so much property be so poor? Land sold for fifty cents an acre at the time because of the republic's remote location, and settlers received thousands of acres free. Immigrants from the U.S came under the sponsorship of the old empresario system. The French settled around Castroville and Germans in towns such as New Braunfels, Indianola, and Fredericksburg. Soldiers also got bounties. Swindlers forged land certificates. The total amount of free land given under grants amounted to nearly 37,000,000 acres.

Turmoil shadowed Houston's second term. News of the failed Santa Fe Expedition started things off. A feud between two groups near the Louisiana border flared over forged land certificates. It resulted in fights, burned homes, and shootings until six hundred troops restored order. Differences between Mexico and Texas also worsened in 1842. Mexican General Rafael Vasquez invaded the Republic because of the Santa Fe affair, retaking San Antonio, Goliad, and Refugio, then withdrawing in a few days as a show of power. This caused war fever as volunteers rushed to San Antonio and urged an invasion of Mexico. Houston feared such a rash act for several reasons. Farmers would need to abandon crops and travel hundreds of miles, which would cause a food shortage the following winter. He also asked how a country of forty thousand could whip a country of six million. Coffers were empty unless a foreign loan came through. (Mexico had the same problem with its continued revolutions and huge army which drained its resources.) Houston vetoed the idea and called for negotiation which angered patriotic settlers.

Houston added kindling to the fire by trying to bring official government papers from Austin to Houston so Indian and Mexican attacks wouldn't destroy them. But Texans in Austin wanted to keep the government archives. Local vigilantes snatched arms and ammunition from the arsenal, followed the loaded wagons, and forced their return to the deserted town. "Poor Austin has sadly changed since you saw it, as indeed, has all the Western part of the Country," a citizen wrote Mirabeau B. Lamar. "We have now but a small population—no business,—& are living under great privations—We have, however, held on to the 'archives,' & will battle for them to the death." This became known as the Archive War. Houston had problems enough with Mexico, hostile Indians, growing debts, feuds, the navy, and efforts to get the U.S. to annex Texas. So he backed off and let documents remain in the deserted town.

THE MIER EXPEDITION

Just as fears calmed down, the Mexicans took San Antonio again, raised their flag, and held the town for over a week. A clash followed near San Antonio, and the Mexicans finally retreated in defeat. Houston then appointed the unpopular General Alexander Somervell to invade Mexico and release prisoners taken from the ill-fated Santa Fe Expedition and recent raids on San Antonio. This offense soured. Some of Somervell's men sacked Laredo, the only town south of the Nueces River and north of the Rio Grande, the extreme frontier area disputed between Mexico and Texas. When Somervell ordered them to return plunder, several hundred men abandoned the offensive. He ordered a retreat, but troops refused and appointed Colonel William S. Fisher as their leader, causing Somervell to return home. Three hundred adventurers, led by Fisher, then attacked Mier, Mexico. As one Texas Ranger recalled: "We were such a bunch of headstrong, foolish men. Many of us were hardly more than boys. We had no common sense. If we had, we would have known that three hundred men were no match for fifteen hundred armed soldiers, supported by cannon. Yet most of us thought we could lick anything."

These "broken down politicians, and adventurers of all sort," as Ranger

Frederick Remington's oil on canvas entitled "The Mier Expedition: The Drawing of the Black Bean"

Samuel H. Walker described many of the band, occupied the town of Mier without resistance. Scouts failed to find any evidence of Mexican soldiers. Fisher took the mayor as hostage and crossed the river again to await reactions. Meanwhile, Mexican infantrymen entered Mier. The impetuous Walker then attacked the town where a bloodied clash followed. Texans might have won the battle, but overestimated the opposing force's strength. So they surrendered and, like the Santa Fe captives, ended up on a forced march to the interior of Mexico.

Some prisoners managed to escape and headed for the mountains where thirst, hunger, and cold weather led to their recapture. Santa Anna, now president again, ordered the infamous Lottery of Death or "Black Bean Incident." One hundred and fifty nine white beans and seventeen black beans were put in an earthen jar. Those who drew the black beans were shot to death. The remaining chained prisoners marched to a barren "hell on earth." This was Perote Prison, south of Mexico City in a barren valley, which also held those captured from San Antonio and the Santa Fe Expedition. Houston, who had opposed this offensive, tried to salvage the situation by signing an armistice which resulted in prisoners eventually being released.

ANSON JONES: ARCHITECT OF ANNEXATION

The last president of the Republic of Texas, Dr. Anson Jones, practiced law and fought at the Battle of San Jacinto before entering politics as secretary of state. He followed Houston's retrenchment policies and marked time until Texas became part of the U.S. As Jones later wrote: "Texas was then a rich jewel lying derelict by the way. She was without a friend who thought her of sufficient consequence to take her by the hand and assist her in her accumulated misfortunes." When James K. Polk won the U.S. presidency over Henry Clay in 1844, the U.S. Congress finally passed a resolution that admitted Texas to statehood following a heated debate regarding the expansion of slavery. This resolution included several conditions: Texas would hold a convention and adopt a new state constitution. It would also cede to the U.S. all fortifications, ports, and harbors, and anything else that related to defense, although it would continue to own all vacant public lands. The U.S. would handle any boundary disputes with other countries. And if Texans desired, they could section the land into several states.

Both England and France still wanted Texas to remain an independent country because of its ports and cotton production. So they urged Mexico to recognize the Republic of Texas. Mexico agreed with one condition: the Republic of Texas couldn't be annexed to the United States. Texas played both ends against the middle in this diplomatic game of high stakes. As Houston told his friend Andrew Jackson: "Texas, with peace, could exist without the United States, but the United States can not without great hazard to the security of their institutions, exist without Texas." But beneath all the bravado, he knew that Texas needed the U.S., which offered a postal system and military protection against Indian raids. Its stable monetary system could also bail out Texas from stifling debts.

When Dr. Anson Jones became the Republic of Texas's last president in 1844, delegates finally convened and approved annexation. The popular vote favored the stars and stripes. U.S. President Polk signed the act on December 28, 1845, and on February 19, 1846, James Pinckney Henderson became the state's first governor. At the inauguration, Jones emoted: "May the Union be perpetual, and may it be the means of conferring benefits and blessings upon the people of all the States, is my ardent prayer. The final act in this great drama is now performed. The Republic of Texas is no more."

The Texas flag became part of this great drama. As a Spanish province, it had flown the Spanish flag, followed by Mexico's cactus and eagle flag.

The 1836 congress had decided that "the National Seal of this Republic shall consist of a single star with the letters 'Republic of Texas' circular on said Seal, which seal shall also be circular." But the 1839 congress decided the star would have "five points, with olive and oak branches encircled and with the letters 'Republic of Texas'." This law changed again the same year, requiring the national arms to be "A white star of five points on an azure ground encircled by an olive and live-oak branch and the letters T-E-X-A-S between the star points; the National Great Seal should bear the Arms of the Nation and the letters 'Republic of Texas' circular." Of course, when Texas became a state, "The Republic of Texas" was replaced by "The State of Texas" which still remains.

In spite of all its troubles, Texas's population mushroomed during the republic years. Anglo Texans grew from 34,000 to over 100,000, while slaves increased from 5,000 to nearly 50,000. (There were also around 300 free slaves in Texas, although few people recognized them.) These figures didn't include Indians. Most *Tejanos* lived around the San Antonio area, retaining political power, their Catholic faith, and Spanish language. Few Texans settled in "no man's land," the frontier region south and west of San Antonio-Goliad because of cattle thieves, Indian raids, and general lawlessness.

Chapter VI

The Damndest Troops in the World

If the enemy oppose my march, in whatever force, I shall fight him."
—General Zachary Taylor

It didn't take long after the annexation of Texas for hostilities to erupt between the U.S. and Mexico. Each country held deep-seated grievances against the other. Some Americans, such as Thomas Jefferson, believed the Louisiana Purchase in 1803 included Texas. The relinquishing of Texas as part of the 1819 Florida Treaty also incensed politicians and many in the West. The *Louisiana Advertiser* ranted, "Texas is worth ten Floridas." Henry Clay bitterly opposed the treaty and called Texas "extremely valuable," praising the fertile soil, climate, and ports on the Gulf of Mexico. Santa Anna had also promised the land in exchange for freedom at San Jacinto. But Mexico insisted that the border belonged at the Nueces River. The expansionist U.S. wanted California before England or France claimed it and also cited defaulted debts as a reason for declaring war. President Polk sent a special envoy, John Slidell, to Mexico City in late 1845 with an offer to pay millions to purchase California and New Mexico. This overture failed because of turmoil in the Mexican government, and Mexican politicians refused to negotiate with the U.S.

Both Mexico and the U.S. overestimated their ability to win a war. Although Mexico boasted a massive army and the advantage of fighting on familiar ground, it suffered from a corrupt and bankrupt government. Squalor and illiteracy were widespread. Timothy J. Henderson says in *A Glorious Defeat* that "family, community, and local political bosses mattered, while the nation as a whole remained a troublesome abstraction." Americans still held grudges over the Alamo, Goliad, raids north of the

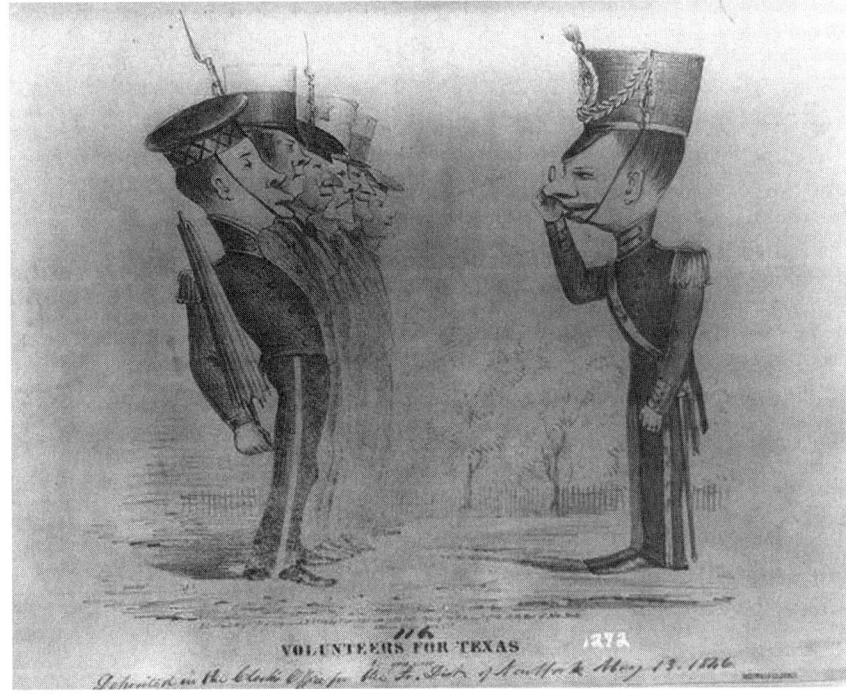

Caricature of volunteers for Texas in the Mexican War, 1846

Rio Grande, and the forced marches of Santa Fe and Mier. They also felt superior to Mexicans. Lt. Ulysses S. Grant claimed that "we are bound to beat the Mexicans whenever and wherever we meet them, no matter how large their numbers." And the age of steam, with its iron horses, magnetic telegraphs, and rise of publishing, offered boundless chances for empire building. Western migration had already started over trails such as the Santa Fe and Camino Real. Yet such naïve optimism ignored the logistics of war with Mexico: the great distances involved, the terrain, the need for a much larger army, and the fact that, except for Indian campaigns, the U.S. hadn't been at war since 1812.

ARMY OF MANIFEST DESTINY

President Polk, who called the U.S. "this heaven-favored land" in his inaugural address, blockaded Mexican gulf ports, and sent General Zachary Taylor, commander of troops in the Southwest, to set up a huge post at Corpus Christi, a small village that mushroomed to several thousand overnight with the usual bars, gambling, and profiteers. Many soldiers suffered from the cold, polluted drinking water, and lack of wood to build fires. In early 1846, Polk moved Taylor to the Rio Grande with orders to defend both Texas and the U.S. in case of Mexican attack. Taylor occupied Point Isabel and the area of present-day Brownsville opposite Matamoros. Mexican cavalry crossed the Rio Grande and trapped a U.S. force, killing or wounding sixteen and taking the rest as prisoners. General Taylor reported that "hostilities may now be considered as commenced."

Polk claimed that Mexico had "shed American blood on American soil" and got a declaration of war from Congress in May of 1846. Meanwhile, Taylor's army won two battles—Palo Alto and Resaca de la Palma—mainly because of superior training and artillery. The U.S. used guns and cannons pulled by horses, while Mexicans used heavy, fixed iron ones that lacked mobility. One surgeon reported, "I saw heads and limbs severed from their bodies and trunks strewed about in awful confusion. Many a body I saw that had been cut in twain … and such ghastly spectacles I hope never to behold again." U.S. soldiers then crossed the Rio Grande and occupied Matamoros after the Mexican general fled.

Texas Rangers took part in these early skirmishes under Taylor, fighting with Colt revolvers and Bowie knives, committing atrocities on Mexicans,

Caricature of early Texas Ranger

The storming of Chapultepec

and refusing to take orders from the army. Yet they prevented Taylor from being trapped at Agua Nueva and urged him to entrench at Buena Vista. Later on they joined General Winfield Scott's forces in the Valley of Mexico, hunting down *guerrilleros* (guerilla soldiers) and causing more trouble with their carousing and hard-boiled tactics. Even old "rough and ready" Taylor rattled: "Them Texas troops are the damndest troops in the world. We can't do without them in a fight, and we can't do anything with them out of a fight."

Once Congress declared war on Mexico in 1846, Taylor moved south with the intent of occupying Monterrey, the key city in northern Mexico. Governor Henderson of Texas got a leave of absence to command volunteers. This fortress in the foothills of the Sierra Madre Range finally fell after U.S. troops breeched the outer works and fought from house-to-house for three days. Taylor agreed to an eight-week truce and Mexican troops withdrew from the city as Americans flew the stars and stripes while singing "Yankee Doodle."

Even though General Taylor made tactical errors, his series of victories led to praise as a national hero and to a congressional gold medal. When he beat Santa Anna at the Battle of Buena Vista, Americans started talking about electing the general as president. He'd not only won engagements but forced Mexicans to retreat nearly five-hundred miles. Differences between Taylor and Polk, however, led to his replacement in the field.

Army of the West

Even before the war with Mexico, both the U.S. and the Republic of Texas wanted the provinces of New Mexico and California, reasons for the ruinous Santa Fe expedition. War invited an invasion of these territories. Colonel Stephen W. Kearny commanded a force that marched over a thousand miles and took Santa Fe in August 1846. He then headed for California over desert and rugged mountain terrain.

Kearny met famed scout Kit Carson who misinformed him that U.S. flags flew everywhere in California. Commodore Sloat had seized Monterrey without a fight, J.C. Fremont beat Northern Mexican forces, and Commodore Robert F. Stockton, who replaced Sloat, entered Los Angeles without resistance and declared himself governor. But Californians revolted and retook Los Angeles, the capital of fifteen hundred inhabitants. Only San Diego remained in U.S. hands.

Clashes flared in both California and New Mexico. Kearny's starved, exhausted troops fought Mexicans at San Pascual on the road to San Diego and suffered serious casualties. One lieutenant recalled: "Our provisions were exhausted, our horses dead, our mules on their last legs and our men ... were ragged, worn down by fatigue and emaciated." But reinforcements arrived and the troops finally gained control of California and areas of New Mexico.

Army of the East

Polk knew Mexico wouldn't surrender unless the U.S. took the capital, Mexico City. He chose General Winfield Scott to command this invasion—the biggest ever undertaken by the U.S. with 8,600 men. Scott's strategy included the following: a siege from Veracruz instead of Monterrey, swiftness to avoid seasonal yellow fever, and an amphibious landing that needed naval support. He landed at Veracruz without opposition and surrounded the city, battering its walls with huge three-ton naval guns that caused civilian casualties before the Mexican army surrendered in March 1847.

Scott then moved north along Mexico's National Highway covering 280 miles between Veracruz and Mexico City, winning victories along the way. During the defeats of Contreras and Churubusco, the U.S. suffered a thousand casualties, and Santa Anna lost one-third of his troops. Santa Anna now suggested an armistice, but hostilities resumed when he violated the agreement, strengthening defenses, and again refusing U.S. territorial demands. As one U.S. captain predicted, "Mexico must fall or we must all find a grave."

Lithograph of scene in Veracruz during the bombardment of 1847

Landing of the American force under General Scott at Veracruz in 1847

Chapter VI: The Damndest Troops in the World

A painting by Adolphe-Jean-Baptiste Bayot entitled "General Scott's Entrance into Mexico"

Scott stormed the Castle of Chapultepec south of Molino del Rey near Mexico City, a bloody battle that left many casualties. After more heavy fighting, Mexico City finally fell when Santa Anna fled, although civilian resistance continued for several days. Militarists praised Scott's victory—outnumbered three to one in a foreign land hundreds of miles away. Santa Anna turned over his command and went into exile again, but would later return to power.

Americans tired of the expensive war and many welcomed its end. The Treaty of Guadalupe Hidalgo finally fixed the Mexican-U.S. border at the Rio Grande. Mexico also ceded New Mexico and most of California, which included what is now Utah—529,017 square miles. They received $15 million for these territories or forty-eight cents per acre. Some questioned the war and land acquisition. Daniel Webster believed California and New Mexico were "not worth a dollar." Although the victory brought prosperity to the U.S.—such as the California gold rush several years later—and helped make the country a world power, it also fueled the slavery debate which resulted in the Civil War. As Ralph Waldo Emerson predicted: "The United States will conquer Mexico, but it will be as the man who swallows the arsenic which brings him down in turn. Mexico will poison us."

LIFE ON THE FRONTIER

The growth of Texas was amazing. In 1821 when Stephen F. Austin arrived in San Antonio, the province included several thousand with two villages, San Antonio and Goliad, besides a few families near the Sabine and Red rivers. This soon grew to around twenty thousand, hardly a threat to the Mexican government. But after annexation, it exploded from 142,000 in 1847 to around 604,000 in 1860. One reason was the Texas Preemption Act of 1854 which gave homesteaders 160 acres of land for around fifty cents an acre. San Antonio became the largest town with a population of 8,000, followed by Galveston and Houston. Austin, the capital, remained a hamlet on the north side of the Colorado River. Other villages remained so small that travelers from the North asked: "Where is the town?" Although most settlers migrated from Southern states, some came from Europe, such as Germans who settled in the New Braunfels-Fredericksburg area. A Frenchman brought 2,000 to the Castroville colony. Other immigrants also arrived looking for a new life in a new state. Most Texas Mexicans, around 5 percent of the population, remained in the south frontier between San Antonio and the Rio Grande.

Hostile Indians discouraged settlement in the state. After the annexation, Texans thought the U.S. government would provide protection against depredations on the frontier. The army did station several thousand soldiers to maintain peace and build a chain of forts across the state, but they couldn't patrol the entire area between the Rio Grande and Nueces Strip. Peace treaties failed to solve the problem, and marauding Indians continued to rustle cattle and horses, raid farms, and take captives. The U.S. tried to put Indians on several reservations, but this failed because of the many different tribes, an unwillingness to farm, and bands that left the reservation to steal and commit violent acts. So the Indian question went unanswered and conflict continued, especially with the warlike Kiowas and Comanches. Several pitched battles resulted, such as John S. "Rip" Ford's 1858 expedition at the Canadian River in Northern Oklahoma.

Sam Houston continued to dominate Texas politics, criticizing senators, disputing the right of the U.S. government to decide Texas boundaries, and maintaining his opposition to talk of secession. When he became governor in 1860, he finally saw a need for frontier protection from unfriendly Indians. He reduced this threat by putting ranger companies along with county militia companies on duty to boost U.S. troops. Secession and the Civil War ended this effort, while Indian strikes later became an even greater danger to frontier expansion.

From can't see to can't see

Because of its vast size, agrarian economy, and weak transportation system, fewer than one thousand manufacturing plants existed in Texas before the Civil War except for scattered grist mills, iron foundries, and sawmills. Most households made their own necessities including shoes and buckskin garments for men. Sam Houston often wore cheap pants and shirts and russet shoes without strings. Cotton remained "king cash" because of the demand in Europe and Northern states. This crop required the use of slave labor. Even Stephen F. Austin realized its importance to the temporary economic success of Texas and wrote his brother in 1835, "Texas must be a slave country. It is no longer a matter of doubt." Slaves also provided planters with both producer's and liquid capital. They not only worked in the cotton, corn, and sugar fields, but could also be mortgaged. The slave population of Texas grew from 30,404 in 1846 to 180,000 in 1860, nearly one-third of the state's population. Most who opposed the system turned their backs.

Plantations thrived between the Red River and mouth of the Nueces River. Slavery didn't spread to the northern and southwestern frontiers for geographical reasons, nor to the far south because of the state's proximity to Mexico, where slaves fled. Slaves (known as bondsmen) did everything from work in the fields to perform skilled occupations and serve as house servants. A few even held managerial jobs such as overseers. Most worked long hours and even tended their own gardens. As one former slave put it, "Us ain't never idle," while another said he labored from "can't see to can't see."

Few planters could afford slaves, only around 30 percent in 1860. Less than 10 percent of the population controlled over 60 percent of slave property. Most farmers raised foodstuffs such as corn, sugar, wheat, and oats. Few traveled anywhere over narrow, dusty roads filled with ruts and tree stumps. Women suffered the most and aged before their time. They married early, bore many children, and worked themselves to death in a society that treated them as inferiors. Wild Indians, the lawless frontier, Mexican armies, and isolation from neighbors also alarmed them. Uprooted immigrant women faced language and cultural barriers. One Texas Ranger-frontiersman remembered that "there was some grounds for the old saying that early Texas was 'hell on women and horses'." Even where there was some help from a few slave women, the duties of the household drained them. "Keeping the home clean, food prepared, washing done, quilts made, rendering the lard when her husband filled hogs, and in the absence of the men, perhaps cutting wood and carrying water as well as looking after the stock about the house, was only a portion of the work of the women along the frontier of central Texas."

Frontier settlers lived in houses made of plain logs with a clapboard door and dirt floor. Wind whistled through cracks in wintertime or during "northers." Furniture was also homemade from trees, sticks, and skins of animals. Fireplaces heated these makeshift buildings. Women cooked either in the fireplace, a separate cook shack, or an extension on the cabin. Children slept on pallets in the loft. Germans preferred stone buildings—many of which still stand in the countryside. Texas Mexicans usually lived in *jacales* covered with grass and adobe mud.

Wealthy merchants and planters, on the other hand, splurged on frame and brick houses with wide halls, high-ceilinged rooms, and verandas. Most chose popular Greek and Georgian styles. Slaves built most of these mansions patterned after those in other Southern states. Owners filled them with fine furniture, brass chandeliers, and marble hearths. Trees, flower gardens, and shrubs beautified the spacious grounds, some sprawling for miles with stock pens and slave quarters. (The governor's mansion in Austin remains one of the elegant buildings constructed during this time.)

Ox trains and cow paths

Most roads between villages remained cow paths before the Civil War started in 1861. Because each county built and maintained its own roads, some just stopped at county lines. People rode horses because of rutted and muddy roads and the lack of bridges across streams and creeks. Ferries carried travelers across key rivers. Stagecoach travel wasn't much better. Passengers helped repair wheels, push vehicles from mud holes, and fight off Indians and robbers along the way. The most famous stage line was the Butterfield Overland Mail Company which passed through Texas on its way from St. Louis and Memphis to San Francisco, and cost from $100 to $200—a lot of money when enlisted privates made $8 a month for army service. The 2,700-mile trip took twenty-four days. Another line called the "jack and mail" used donkeys to carry mail across the mountains. Freight haulers chose mules or ox-drawn wagons with iron wheels five or six feet high to carry cotton and heavy goods. *Tejano* teamsters operated many teams.

River trade in the state also presented barriers such as sandbars, log jams, and low water levels. Some boats got stuck in the shallows and remained grounded until spring floods, while others were abandoned. Rafts could transport cotton down rivers but boats couldn't return upstream. A few steamboats, however, managed to navigate difficult Texas waterways. King Ranch founder, Richard King, who floated cotton down the Rio Grande during the Civil War and then invested in land and cattle, started his illustrious career at this time with a steamboat.

BOOKS, BITTERS, AND BIBLES

The lack of transportation influenced education, entertainment, and religion. Farmers couldn't afford books and needed children at home to help with chores. The few who did attend school walked for miles or rode on horseback. Money was scarce because Texas lacked a banking system, so few farmers spent much on extras taken for granted today. Churches gradually became the center of social life in rural communities with the help of missionaries.

Stephen F. Austin sought public education early as 1823. The constitution of 1845 provided that one-tenth of revenue from taxes should be used for free public schools, but few opened because of an indifference to education. In 1850 only one child in five or six attended school, mostly one-room buildings with seats made of split logs. One pioneer teacher in the 1850s said of her classroom: "It has one door and a window without sash or glass. But there is no lack of ventilation, the spaces between the logs admitting lots of air." Spiders, scorpions, and snakes also came in through those spaces and terrified students. Some classes met outside under trees.

In 1854, Governor Pease's administration passed a law that set aside $2 million from U.S. indemnity bonds to maintain common schools. Again several counties responded because they lacked local taxes to build schoolhouses and provide needed equipment. Yet a few schools managed to survive. San Antonio opened a public school system in 1853, using earlier funds provided by the Mexican government. German settlements and fraternal organizations also supported free schools.

Youngsters from wealthy families attended private schools, enjoyed tutors and governesses, or went to other states for their education. Academies required strict discipline and offered classical languages such as Latin, Greek, and Hebrew as well as declamation, natural philosophy, and ancient history. Newspaper ads stressed rules such as "a strict discipline rigidly enforced" and "course of study full, instruction thorough, and discipline strict." Some schools separated boys and girls into different departments, offering girls "ornamental" courses such as art and music. One Texan recalled attending the first school he'd "seen or heard of that dispensed with the rod" and that classes included "grammar, history, geometry and surveying" as well as Latin.

Although few Texans went to school, many apparently learned to read. Over 70 newspapers reached a circulation of almost 100,000 before the Civil War, the most notable being the *Telegraph* and *Texas Register*. Most were weeklies, four pages long, and covered local news and horse racing. Subscribers sometimes paid in beeswax, cotton, or poultry. Bartering typified the economy. (Even Mirabeau Lamar gave 500 acres for a horse.) Books on travel, history, and personal journals also appeared at this time.

Frontier hardships hindered farmers from not only getting an education but also from enjoying entertainments except an occasional wedding, funeral, or public hanging. Males hunted, fished, and competed in corn shuckings and log rollings. In the more populated areas, people attended barbecues, county and state fairs, parades, and watched horse races and rooster duels. Whiskey and gambling boomed in saloons. One native later remembered: "Dancing parties were common everywhere, and were considered by the young and even the middle aged person as being occasions of the greatest pleasure. Quiltings were common … The boys played ball, while the men engaged in wrestling, jumping and foot races … Often times there were shooting matches. These simple entertainments drew a great many people together."

The small elite class, mostly plantation owners, attended ballroom dances and plays, and belonged to clubs. In Galveston, for example, they stayed at the Tremont Hotel where they could drink alcoholic beverages such as "iced mint-julip … a glass of Madiera and bitters." Then they retired to the dining room for dinner. The rich also traveled by steamboat to New Orleans where they shopped and attended cultural events. Rutherford B. Hayes found "no end of entertainment" in Texas where guests traveled for miles to hospitable plantation houses filled with "merriment and dancing until 4:30 a.m."

Like its educational system, churches got a slow start in Texas and viewed idle pleasures with a jaundiced eye. In 1839 a Houston paper noted that the town had a courthouse, theatre, jail and a capitol—but not one church. The Methodist Church organized in 1840 and the Baptists followed in 1848. Few colonists except *Tejanos* practiced Catholicism. Churches sponsored picnics, charities, bazaars, and Sunday schools, and tried to instill moral values such as temperance. Sam Houston spoke to the first meeting of the Temperance Union and confessed: "Do as I say, not as I have done."

Border bandits, frontier lawlessness, and brutal Comanche attacks—coupled with the burning slavery question—led many Texans to doubt the Union's interest in Southern causes. The election of Republican Abraham Lincoln as president worsened these concerns. Then South Carolina seceded from the Union. Texas followed in January 1861 and Civil War engulfed the entire country.

Chapter VII

The Wild Ravings of Fanatics

"All I ask is that you keep up with the Texans!"
—General Robert E. Lee

Texas was now on the move. It produced over a million and a half bushels of wheat, sixteen million bushels of corn, and 430,000 bales of cotton a year—all made possible by slavery. Talk even spread of reopening the African slave trade because of the thriving plantation system, which enabled the rich to control most of the state's political power and economic prosperity. So slaves, making up around 30 percent of the population, remained vital to continued growth. Their total value was enormous since the average slave sold for around $1,000.

TEXAS WITHDRAWS FROM THE UNION

With so much at stake, opposition to the anti-slavery Union inflamed Texans. People held parades and torchlight demonstrations. Some even wanted Texas to become an independent republic once again. Governor Sam Houston, however, considered secession treason and spoke out against "the wild ravings of fanatics," insisting that Texans must "maintain the Constitution and stand by the Union." He warned about civil war and bloodshed. Houston predicted that the Union would blockade the coast, take New Orleans and the Mississippi River, cut the Confederacy in half, and make the South lose English and French support—all prophetic remarks. Jefferson Davis and Robert E. Lee felt likewise but supported the Southern cause.

Bitterness between the North and South continued to deepen over states rights and the slavery question. Quarrels broke out in Kansas. Politicians debated the problem while Southerners started talking secession. In 1859, John Brown spearheaded a raid on Harper's Ferry which failed, as did Juan Cortina's attack at Brownsville. Comanche raids also terrified Texas frontier towns. Lincoln's election in 1860 over the National Democratic Party's candidate, Stephen A. Douglas, led people to believe he would oppose slavery and seek internal improvement programs, a view that many Texans supported.

Six weeks after the election, South Carolina seceded from the union. Five other slave states soon followed: Mississippi, Florida, Alabama, Georgia, and Louisiana. Leaders from each state met in Montgomery, Alabama, and elected Jefferson Davis president of the Confederacy and Alexander H. Stephens vice president. They modeled a Provisional Constitution on the Constitution of the United States, believing that government should rest on the consent of the governed, and planned to send several delegates to Washington, D.C., in hopes of resolving political differences.

Prominent Texans opposed old-line conservative Houston and asked him to convene either the legislature or call a convention to address the issue of secession from the Union. Some held mass meetings. Others drafted letters and petitions and distributed pamphlets. Houston issued an Address to the People of Texas in which he called for reason and good sense, while secession leaders printed in newspapers their own address, asking for the election of state delegates to attend a state convention in early 1861. Houston, in turn, called a special session which the legislature ignored. So he preached again, trying to forestall the inevitable, but public sentiment overshadowed caution. When the legislature met, it resolved that Texas should withdraw from the Union on March 2, 1861—twenty-five years after the state became a republic. The ordinance passed 166 to 8. Voters supported the convention's decision: 46,129 for secession and 14,697 against it.

Even before the popular vote, the convention decided to join the Confederate States of America and drew up a declaration of causes for leaving the Union. Houston called secession unconstitutional and agreed with some that Texas should become an independent nation once again. The convention passed an ordinance that all state officers take an oath of allegiance to the Confederacy. When Houston refused, the convention declared the office of governor vacant and appointed Edward Clark as governor. The impassioned Houston told the convention, "I love Texas too well to bring civil strife and bloodshed upon her. To avert this calamity, I shall make no endeavor to maintain my authority as Chief Executive of this State, except by the peaceful exercise of my functions ... but still claiming that I am its Chief Executive." When Lincoln offered to send troops, Houston declined after conferring with friends, and retired from public service.

FIGHTING ON THE FRONT

Before Texas officially seceded from the Union, it appointed a committee to assume all Union posts in the state. Ben McCullough, Texas Ranger and Mexican War hero, became military commander of the commission. He quickly asked for the surrender of all arms and munitions at army headquarters in San Antonio, housed in the historic Alamo. Its commander, General David Twiggs, a Georgian, failed to receive directives from Washington and therefore ordered the evacuation of forts and garrisons controlled by U.S. soldiers.

INDIAN RAIDS

The withdrawal of 2,700 Union army troops from the Texas frontier left it open to looting and pillaging from Kiowa-Comanche Indians who attacked at will. They also paralyzed the Santa Fe Trail, preventing foodstuffs from reaching Denver and other outposts. President Lincoln even offered pardons to any tribes who stopped harassing wagon trains and

Engraving from Harper's Weekly *entitled "Surrender of General Twiggs to Texan Troops"*

supported the Union. Posses and militia lacked the experience to cope with such attacks. Many Texas settlers "forted up" in stockades, while others abandoned homes, leaving remote areas desolate.

Although the Confederacy at first expressed concern over this frontier crisis, Texas Rangers ended up trying to patrol hundreds of miles without adequate mounts, provisions, or ammunition. By 1863 raiding parties increased in the northwestern counties. Over three hundred Comanches attacked farms and ranches across the Red River, driving off ten thousand head of cattle in 1863-64 alone. They killed, burned homes, and kidnapped women and children. At Elm Creek, warriors savaged settlers. A lucky bullet, however, killed Little Buffalo, and the Comanches withdrew. Troops gave up the chase after a hundred miles. In 1864 Colonel Christopher "Kit" Carson fought a thousand Kiowas at the first battle of Adobe Walls, north of the Canadian River, and retreated when the Indians set fire to the tall grass and endangered his rear guard.

The Elmo Creek raid and other atrocities fueled hatred of the Indians among Texans, which led to an unfortunate battle with peaceful Kickapoos traveling to Mexico in early 1865. Indian scouts saw hundreds at Dove Creek, near the Concho, and Confederates attacked without a plan, specific orders, or reconnaissance. The Indians sought cover in a brush thicket and beat off the Confederates in a crossfire maneuver, shooting them one at a time, which led to a panic and more than forty casualties.

The New Mexico Campaign

Confederates also launched an abortive attempt to seize the American Southwest in 1861-62. Such an invasion, on the surface, offered long-range benefits. It would increase the land area of the South and give access to 1,200 miles of Pacific coastline. The control of gold and silver mines in Arizona, Nevada, and California promised credit abroad, as well as increased respect from needed European powers. Annexing some Mexican states could prove an astute strategy and provide an unlimited source of food and supplies for the frenzied Confederacy. Lieutenant Colonel John R. Baylor and General Henry H. Sibley led these failed offensives.

Baylor's force swept into New Mexico. He claimed part of the region, calling it Arizona, and made himself military governor. This territory was part of over 500,000 square miles the U.S. received from the Mexican War. The offensive's main objective? To use barren New Mexico as a stepping stone to California with its seaports and rich agricultural resources.

Meanwhile, General Sibley received orders from Confederate President Jefferson Davis to raise a brigade in San Antonio to invade New Mexico.

CHAPTER VII: The Wild Ravings of Fanatics 81

This offensive took more time to launch than expected, and the self-sustaining expedition started in late fall. After tramping around seven hundred miles, Sibley won the bloody battle of Valverde, then pushed on to Albuquerque and Santa Fe. But bad weather, short supplies, and an enemy both in front and behind them sabotaged the attack. They, likewise, failed to consider Union reinforcements from Colorado and California. Natives also seemed indifferent to the cause.

Losing a supply train at the furious Battle of Glorieta Pass forced Sibley's return to Texas. The grueling journey back to San Antonio took months. Instead of using the river road, Sibley chose a route filled with steep canyons and arroyos. Rations and water ran short. Hostile Apache Indians harassed the weak and sick soldiers. Order finally collapsed among troops. Only a handful of wagons and 1,500 men from the original 2,500 force remained.

Thus ended the South's grandiose plan. Success in the New Mexico campaign would have brought Sibley great honor and changed the entire path of the Civil War. He blamed defeat on lack of support from superiors and inadequate war supplies because merchants refused to accept Southern money. Trying to salvage a scarred career, he blustered that the whole area wasn't "worth a quarter of the blood and treasure expended on its conquest."

By the time Sibley's battered troops returned to San Antonio, the Confederacy had reeled from a series of military blows. They lost Fort Henry and Fort Donelson in Tennessee, fought the brutal Battle of Pea Ridge, and surrendered New Orleans to the Union. At least General Robert E. Lee managed to save Richmond. The clash between blues and grays continued to rage throughout the South.

COASTAL DEFENSE

Although offensives against Indians on the frontier and the New Mexico expedition fell short, home defense against Union attempts to secure gulf ports went well—mainly the recapture of Galveston, the Battle of Sabine Pass, and attempts to take Brownsville and control of the Red River.

The Union needed part of the Gulf Coast to control blockade running and serve as a base for operations in the region. Galveston, the second largest city and principal port on the Texas coast, fell into their hands in 1862 when Unionists entered the harbor and asked for the city's surrender, which defenders accepted. But this island occupancy lasted a short while. Outraged Confederate leaders replaced Galveston's commander with John

Engraving from Harper's Weekly *of Confederate ironclads at Galveston*

B. Magruder, who saw the importance of taking the city, and began recruiting troops. The Union commander, believing a few vessels could protect the town, failed to destroy the two-mile railroad bridge that connected mainland Texas with the island.

On New Year's Day, 1863, Magruder attacked Galveston. Two cottonclad steamers (ships that used pressed bales of cotton as armor) reinforced troops. Mayhem followed. Cannon balls, grape shot, and splinters filled the air. "The heavens were in a blaze," reported one doctor. "Musketry and heavy guns ... roaring, rushing, and finally exploding in the air or on the vessels ... The wounded began to come in very soon afterward." Confederates finally rammed and boarded the famed warship *Harriet Lane*, killing most officers and forcing the crew to surrender. During a short ceasefire to help the wounded on both sides, remaining Union vessels escaped to sea, leaving the battered, fishhook-shaped island once again secure in Texas hands. The defeat dazed Union militarists, who considered Galveston's importance on the Gulf Coast only second to Mobile and New Orleans. Admiral David Farragut called it the "most unfortunate" and "most shameful" incident in the navy's entire history.

President Lincoln, concerned about French presence in Mexico, needed control of some Texas port. The military under General Nathaniel P. Banks targeted Sabine Pass between Texas and Louisiana. Its capture would curtail cotton trade with Mexico and open the way for other assaults near Houston. Five thousand troops supported by eighteen transports, four gunboats, fifty wagons and ambulances, and hundreds of horses and mules landed at Sabine Pass to secure a beachhead at Fort Griffin on the mud and salt flats. But the fleet missed the entrance and steamed nearly to Galveston before turning around, thus losing the crucial element of surprise darkness offered. This forced them to make new plans. Instead of landing troops first, gunboats would shell the fort, and leave mop-up operations to the infantry.

Rather than surrender the fort, former Houston saloonkeeper Dick Dowling waited for the warships to get within stake range before firing on them. Only forty-two men won the battle in less than an hour. His force disabled two of the gunboats, splintering wood and ripping open boilers, which led the other two gunboats to back down the channel. Union losses included hundreds killed, wounded, and taken prisoner, while defenders of Fort Griffin only suffered powder burns from the overheated guns. As Dowling later said, "Our motto was 'Victory or death.'" This clash ended the Union's attempt to control the Sabine Pass area.

After the Union defeat at Sabine Pass, General Banks launched several other offenses in the fall of 1863—the successful lower Texas coast attack and the Red River expedition, which ruined his military career. A fleet took Brazos Island near the mouth of the Rio Grande in early November and moved upstream to Brownsville. The area commander panicked and gave orders to destroy all moveable supplies in the vicinity. After his evacuation, a huge explosion of powder burned Fort Brown, several blocks of the town, and set fire to a ferry carrying women and children across the Rio Grande to Matamoros. Looters also stripped buildings of valuables.

The Union occupation of Brownsville failed to end the cotton traffic, which just moved up river, although General Banks captured other cities along the coast such as Corpus Christi, Aransas Pass, and Indianola. This led Confederate General Magruder to send John S. "Rip" Ford to regain

Engraving from Harper's Weekly *of Union soldiers occupying Brownsville*

control of the lower Rio Grande. Ford had done everything from being a physician to serving in the Texas House of Representatives and editing the *Texas Democrat*. He was also a former Texas Ranger. When Ford reached Brownsville, Unionists had abandoned the area except for twelve hundred troops at Brazos Island, as they regrouped for another massive attack—this time on northeast Louisiana and eastern Texas.

Union General Banks then moved up the Red River, which runs from northern Texas through the southern tip of Arkansas and then down Louisiana to New Orleans, with thirty thousand troops, the largest inland gunboat offensive during the war. He wanted to gain control of Shreveport, secession capital of Louisiana and headquarters of the Trans-Mississippi Department of the Confederacy, in order to launch attacks against the interior of Texas. Banks' immense force moved along a narrow inland route while a flotilla sailed up the Red River. A third force came from Arkansas to complete this operation, which could also seize a fortune in cotton along the river.

Confederate troops met the Unionists at Mansfield, around forty miles south of Shreveport, and forced them back to Pleasant Hill. A bloodbath followed in which both sides suffered heavy casualties. Union soldiers retreated in disorder and lost most of their train and artillery. Then the Red River failed to flood as planned and forced navy ships to paddle backwards downstream while snipers damaged most of their craft before they reached New Orleans. The Arkansas troops also nearly starved because of exhausted supplies and lost a supply train of two hundred wagons.

The Red River campaign resulted in around ten thousand losses to both sides and left a trail of burned homes, barns, and mills. One cavalryman compared the land to "a perfect forest of blackened chimneys" and added that "ruin and desolation is stamped upon the whole face of the country." President Lincoln relieved General Banks of field command, ending his famed army career. Although neither side claimed victory, the Confederacy had kept the Union from taking northern Louisiana and eastern Texas.

BEHIND THE LINES

Although the war disrupted life in Texas, the state was spared from major Union invasions except on the coastal regions. Louisiana stood at its eastern boundary, Indian territory in the north, and rugged terrain on the western border. Despite this insulation from the threat of Union attacks, times remained tough. Supplies of goods such as salt (used for preserving meat), coffee, sugar, and medicines remained critical because of the Union blockade. Prices soared. Iron shot went from $25 a ton to $1,500, salt from $.65 a sack to $8, corn from $.67 a bushel to $25, sugar up to $75 a pound, and flour $1,200 a barrel. One woman stood in line for hours to purchase a bolt of domestic cloth, a pair of shoes, and a dozen candles for a staggering $180. A private's $11 a month salary couldn't buy a pound of bacon. One Southern journal printed an illustration of a woman going to market with her money in a wheelbarrow and leaving with a small handbag of goods.

While sixty to seventy thousand males trudged off to war, women tried to keep the home fires burning. Some cut up carpets for blankets and used pages from old books and wallpaper scraps for letters and envelopes. They made clothes from curtains, sheets, and pillow shams, and bandages from scraps of cloth. Buttons and shoes were carved from wood. Nails, stray pins, and kettles were reworked into war materials. One woman remembered: "A needle dropped or misplaced was searched for hours; if one was broken its irreparable loss was lamented."

Many women worked farms and plantations, helped by children and slaves. They planted a cotton patch, sorghum field, and even plowed with oxen. Others took up knitting and spinning, raised livestock, and fought Indians. Some women and children labored in factories making powder, caps, and cartridges. One woman recalled: "The first of the war I made a good garden and planted about half an acre of corn, all of which I worked myself. Many times whilst at work I would be so hot and tired that I would cry like a child … This garden was a great help to my family and I sold several dollars worth of vegetables. I also raised one hundred chickens which was a great help in hard times."

In addition to domestic and plantation tasks, women also served in other ways that not only made them stronger but reshaped their identities. Some took teaching jobs left vacant by males. Others attended the sick in hospital wards and formed Ladies Aid Societies that made bandages and other needed items. Relief committees also helped the families of servicemen. The rich in Texas as well as other Southern states gave generously to such causes. Churches, likewise, raised funds and helped the poor. A few women even freighted cotton and acted as spies.

Slaves, for the most part, remained peaceful during the war, partly due to loyalty and partly due to the failure of Union troops to penetrate the state, although some fled to Mexico. Arkansas, Louisiana, and Missouri "refugeed" thousands of bondsmen from Texas. General Magruder also used bondsmen to build fortifications, railroads, and other public service projects. Yet Texans still feared uprisings after the 1860 insurrection in which slaves of Union sympathizers set fires in towns and cities, causing a million dollars in damage. Some were hanged. Mobs also horsewhipped and hanged abolitionists caught supplying slaves with poison and firearms.

Union sympathizers undercut Texas during the entire Civil War. Authorities also felt many Mexicans along the Rio Grande in south Texas would turn hostile in a Union attack because they opposed slavery and didn't have any stake in the conflict. The disaffected also included wealthy landowners and important political figures. Sam Houston retired and never took the oath of allegiance to the Confederacy. Former Governor E. M. Pease also withdrew from practicing law during the bitter war. Former militant Texas congressman A. J. Hamilton fled to Washington where he was appointed brigadier general and military governor of Texas, and south Texas judge Edmund J. Davis later became reconstruction governor of Texas. As the war progressed, dissent increased because of impressments, taxes, and high casualties among those who fought outside the state.

Rebellious groups of pro-Union Texans called meetings and defied authorities. Some formed secret associations. Draftees refused to answer the Confederate call or be sworn into military service. Others got exemptions from doctors, joined a home guard, or volunteered for frontier defense service. Southern loyalists, of course, considered such Texans traitors and supporters of Lincoln. They detained individuals, infiltrated groups, and tried to crack down on ringleaders and Union sympathizers. Two results of such opposing belief systems became known as the "Battle of the Nueces" and "The Great Hanging at Gainesville."

Around twenty thousand Germans settled in the south-central part of Texas before the Civil War and became influential in towns such as New Braunfels and Fredericksburg. But their culture differed in several ways, such as opposing slavery and siding with the North. Some even resisted the draft and sent a petition to the U.S. Congress that expressed such sentiments, while others around Fredericksburg formed a Loyal Union League. During the summer of 1862, a group of German Texans left for Mexico, planning to join Union forces, but Confederate troops tracked them to the Nueces River where the surprised Germans suffered casualties.

The "great hanging" at Gainesville involved several northern counties near the Red River settled by farmers and mechanics with few slaves who also remained Union loyalists. They resisted conscription laws that allowed substitutes and excluded anyone who managed twenty or more slaves from serving in the war. One doctor remembered that just mentioning the Conscript Law "was like a spark lighting on powder; all was in a blaze of opposition, as deep and as fierce as it was possible for it to exist in the human mind was plainly manifested." Leaders of this order planned a Peace Party Plot that involved rising against Texans, parceling out property, and killing women and children whom they considered inferior.

This plot led to charges of conspiracy and insurrection. Numerous arrests followed. A mob met outside the Gainesville courthouse and chose a citizen's court comprised of slaveholders who hanged over forty men, some innocent. Several nearby counties also took similar actions fueled by other fears that included Indian raids, slave rebellion, and a Union invasion. Such frightful acts helped to divide rather than unite north Texas in a common cause.

Meanwhile, economic conditions worsened as the value of paper money hit bottom, along with that of bonds and treasury notes. Texas had few cash reserves and lacked an industrial base. Scattered small factories made wagons, saddles, and leather goods. The military board set up a few iron foundries and a textile factory at the state penitentiary at Huntsville, but many chartered projects never got off the ground. But Texas held an ace in the hole—plenty of cotton to exchange for medicines, munitions, and domestic goods in Mexico and abroad.

COTTON AND THE BLOCKADE RUNNERS

Shortly after the evacuation of Fort Sumter, President Lincoln declared a blockade of all Southern ports to choke trade with outside markets. This task became impractical with around 3,500 miles of seacoast to patrol—especially as the Union owned less than a hundred warships, some old and in bad repair, others cruising abroad, and only a handful ready for action. These vessels also drew too much water to enter shallow Southern ports, and new steamships burned too much coal. So the military focused on main eastern seaboard ports with rail connections vital to the Confederacy. Gunboats also combed the Mississippi River. When Vicksburg fell in 1863, the North succeeded in cutting the Confederacy in two, which left parts of Louisiana, Missouri, and all of Texas isolated, causing severe shortages of food and supplies. For the most part, however, the early blockade caught only one in four or five ships.

Smuggling and blockade running boomed in southern Texas because of the 1848 Treaty of Guadalupe-Hildago which stated that both Mexico and the U.S. were free to use the Rio Grande. Confederate boats flew the Mexican flag and put ownership in the names of Mexican friends to avoid seizure by the navy. Illicit trade even flourished with Northern merchants. Over 800,000 bales of cotton reached New York, more than combined shipments to England and France. In turn, New York's exports averaged around one million dollars a week, including everything from war supplies to silks and spirits.

Brownsville and Matamoros, twin border towns on either side of the Rio Grande near the Gulf of Mexico, became the South's lifeline and the backdoor of the Confederacy. One teamster later recalled "a never ending stream of cotton pouring into Brownsville." When he crossed into Mexico, he saw "ox trains, mule trains, and trains of Mexican carts, all laden with cotton coming from almost every town in Texas." While hundreds of wagons brought cotton to the Texas coast, some carried army supplies and other goods north for Confederate use.

Matamoros, Mexico, became one of the world's leading shipping ports and center for diplomatic exchanges, especially after the Union blockade of Brazos Santiago in 1863. Its population mushroomed as streets filled with agents, swindlers, and speculators from the North, South, England, France, and Germany. One officer wrote: "Matamoros is to the rebellion west of the Mississippi what New York is to the United States."

Mexico, of course, also benefited from the cotton trade, although internal political conflicts between the government and invasion by France at the time created an explosive situation. Attacks, street fighting, and looting typified Matamoros for most of the Civil War as revolutionaries tried to gain control of the city. Mexico's growing textile industries needed cotton, which Texas could supply in abundance. Duties were also collected from every shipment of goods transported through Matamoros. In addition, the border states sought Confederate support against the central Mexican government.

Because the inadequate Texas railroad line ended at Alleyton (near Houston), teamsters laboriously hauled cotton by mules and ox-cart freight wagons hundreds of miles from as far away as Louisiana, Arkansas, and Missouri to the lower Rio Grande Valley through semi-arid and desert country filled with bandits, hostile Indians, and bushwackers. Many animals died from exhaustion and lack of water. The Richard King ranch became an official cotton depot where teamsters stored cotton and bought supplies for the remaining 125 miles to Brownsville. Another route went from Alleyton to San Antonio and then south to King's ranch. Cotton was then ferried to Matamoros and down the Rio Grande to Bagdad, Mexico, on small steamers.

Bagdad stood at the mouth of the Rio Grande. Once vessels reached the former shanty town, ocean-going ships from European ports waited offshore for lighter vessels to carry out the cotton and exchange it for goods. Neutrality laws prevented Union ships from stopping the lucrative trade at the Gulf's mouth, although they delayed some foreign ships, which caused protests and brought British men-of-war into the western Gulf to protect their interests.

COLLAPSE OF THE CONFEDERACY

Even though blockade running helped Texans get goods needed to fight, economic conditions worsened in the Confederacy. Money grew nearly worthless while prices kept rising. The North possessed superior manufacturing, railroads, and natural resources. Texas interest in the war crumbled as it dragged on instead of ending in a few months. A gradual decline in food crops also affected the home front, along with heavy taxes, and an increasing number of casualties. This led to massive desertions—sometimes as much as one-fourth to one-half of companies—as soldiers returned to their destitute families. Some Texans began calling the conflict "a rich man's war but a poor man's fight."

On April 9, 1865, General Robert E. Lee surrendered the Army of Northern Virginia at Appomattox Court House, followed by the exchange of prisoners and weapons. Other Southern generals soon did likewise. Texas responded with defiance. Kirby Smith, commander of the Trans-Mississippi department, John Magruder, Confederate commander in Texas, and Governor Pendleton Murrah all exhorted Texans to keep fighting. Others urged guerilla warfare.

A month earlier, famed General Lew Wallace (later author of *Ben Hur*) had traveled to Brazos Santiago with a plan to help Texans save face and repel the French and imperialists from Mexico. He suggested that they surrender and reenter the Union with honor, which included keeping arms and driving rebels out of Mexico. "Rip" Ford liked the idea, but it fell through.

Union troops, meanwhile, advanced on Texans near Brownsville at Palmito Ranch. When Unionists tried to overrun "Rip" Ford's force, he shouted: "Men we have whipped the enemy in all our previous fights! We can do it again!" Union soldiers broke ranks and fled. This last land fight of the Civil War happened one month after Lee's surrender.

Once Texans accepted defeat, troops disbanded and returned home, some looting the countryside because they hadn't been paid for months. Riots broke out in Galveston, San Antonio, Austin, and other towns. Robbers broke into government warehouses and even the bankrupt state treasury. After Lincoln's assassination on April 15, 1865, President Andrew

Engraving of the Battle of Palmito Ranch, the last conflict of the Civil War

Johnson demanded that all traitors hang. As a result, General Kirby Smith and General Magruder fled to Mexico. So did "Rip" Ford and former governors Pendleton Murrah and Edward Clark. During the spring of 1865, Texas lacked a government. One noted planter mourned that "the army has entirely disbanded & are sacking as they go … We have no Govt. or country. God help us."

But the worst was yet to come—reconstruction.

CHAPTER VIII

A Conquered Province

"You cannot pick up a paper in East Texas without reading of murder, assassinations, and robbery." —Cincinnati Commercial (1869)

Southern leaders lacked a blueprint for demobilization after the war. The Union sent home around 800,000 troops within six months after the surrender at Appomattox, most on railroad cars under a highly ordered military command. The few Southern railroads that remained intact used different gauges. Weary Confederate soldiers, many penniless, scattered and used any means possible to travel—some walking barefooted for hundreds of miles over dusty roads. They slept on the ground and asked for food along the way. "I have worn my last gray jacket," one soldier said at the journey's end. "I have fired my last shot for Dixie."

Texas suffered far less than Confederate states east of the Mississippi, as its interior towns and farms remained. But many endured hardships and lost sons. Casualties included a quarter of the state's white male population. The war also disrupted agricultural trade. Still a rural culture—95 percent of the people lived on farms or in small towns—the state now lacked slaves to harvest cotton, its main crop. Money was worthless and bank stocks depleted. The use of gold helped soften financial losses somewhat. However, the state government was broke which caused many small farmers to despair. As one soldier later wrote: "When I came home from the army, I had no money—no clothes … Before I went to the army I had bought a house for $3000—paid $1500—and owed the balance—so when I was done soldiering—I had nothing but a wife and four children and a house with something like about $2200 due on it. My Negroes had all been freed & they were poorer than I was. Two of the men wanted

The Freedmen's Bureau tried to mediate between blacks and Anglos

to stay with me, and work on as they had been—but I would not permit them. I could not afford to do it."

JUNETEENTH AND THE FREEDMEN'S BUREAU

As part of President Andrew Johnson's Reconstruction plan, General Philip Sherman became commander of the Military Division of the Southwest with headquarters in New Orleans. He sent General Gordon Granger and 1,800 men to Galveston, while thousands of others went to the Rio Grande to demonstrate against the French in Mexico. Granger's general order declared that "all slaves are free." Black Texans still celebrate June 19, 1865, as "Juneteenth." Emancipation was one thing but equal rights another. By the Civil War's end, the Texas slave population had increased to around 250,000, partly because of refugees from Arkansas and Louisiana. Unfortunately, neither Lincoln nor Johnson provided for blacks as part of reconstruction. Johnson believed that states should control their own destinies, which explains his generous policy toward the conquered South. Desperate for labor to harvest crops, some planters offered food and clothing for work, which many freedmen rejected. Thousands wandered along roads, begging, doing odd jobs, and stealing to keep alive. A federal agency called the Freedmen's Bureau arose to help blacks make the transition from slavery to freedom. General E. J. Gregory directed the Texas branch, which offered relief to the needy. It tried to enforce fairness in labor contracts, reduce violence, and intervene in court cases involving blacks. The Bureau also set up schools to educate blacks. Insufficient funds and staff crippled the program which ended in 1870.

Unrest and violence spread during Reconstruction. General Sheridan said that if he owned both hell and Texas, he "would rent Texas out and live in hell." Organizations like the Freedmen's Bureau lacked resources to police the state and clashed with defiant citizens who resented its presence. On the frontier, Comanches attacked and murdered farmers. Misfits, cutthroats and outlaws robbed, terrorized towns, and stole livestock. The Ku Klux Klan, dressing in long flowing white robes and tall hoods, harassed blacks to keep them from the polls and enjoying basic civil liberties. Bitter Southern conservative groups formed democratic clubs to threaten and coerce Unionists, which nearly escalated into a "New Rebellion" or race war. Between 1865 and 1868, nearly a thousand people were murdered in the state.

BARRIERS TO RECONSTRUCTION

Politicians, as well as militarists, faced numerous barriers in their attempt to reorganize the Texas government—mainly bickering among Unionists and secessionists with different agendas for the state's future. President Johnson appointed Andrew J. Hamilton provisional governor, who soon convened a constitutional convention to select delegates. Members cancelled all state debts, the ordinance of secession, and recognized the abolishment of slavery. But they refused to ratify the Thirteenth Amendment to the Constitution of the U.S. and denied blacks the right to vote, to hold office, and to testify in court cases that involved whites.

An election followed. Most Democrats couldn't vote because of their allegiance to the South, now prohibited by law. So the Republicans split into two factions. They nominated Unionist Elisha M. Pease and conservative James W. Throckmorton for governor. The main party difference? Throckmorton opposed black suffrage, while Pease supported voting rights for literate black males. The vote favored Throckmorton four to one because of his appeal to ex-secessionists and those who opposed any radical change in government. When he took office in August 1866, Pres-

Reconstruction photo of the Alamo being used for storage

ident Johnson declared an end to the Texas rebellion and returned control to civil authorities—even though some had earlier supported secession.

Governor Throckmorton wanted to restore prewar politics dominated by rich planters. The new legislature, therefore, elected two secessionists to the U.S. Senate whom politicians in Washington snubbed. Then it refused to ratify the Thirteenth Amendment (abolition of slavery) and Fourteenth Amendment (guaranteed rights for U.S. citizenship). The legislature also passed "black codes" that prohibited freedmen from serving on juries, holding office, voting, getting an education, and marrying whites. Fines and contract laws allowed employers to regulate and control their lives. At any rate, many blacks were treated badly during the late 1860s. Tensions crackled between the two races. Churches and schools were burned. The discriminatory Homestead Law prevented blacks from becoming landowners, nor could they secure credit at banks. So most remained tenants and worked for between $30 and $60 a year. Although Texas eventually allowed blacks citizenship in the Union, politicians planned to later strip them of any civil rights.

Congress, in turn, passed Reconstruction Acts that made Texas a "conquered province" under military rule. It divided the South into five military districts and in 1867 appointed distinguished Union General Philip Sheridan (who supported the Reconstruction policies of radical Republicans) commander of Texas and Louisiana. He took immediate action, prohibiting Governor Throckmorton from holding any elections or making appointments to empty vacancies in elective offices. Jurors had to sign an oath that they hadn't abetted the Confederacy—which eliminated many Texans from public service. Other restrictions followed. The general then removed Throckmorton from office, calling him "an impediment to reconstruction," and reappointed earlier Governor Elisha M. Pease.

A constitutional convention met in June 1868 in which Republicans dominated the floor, many of them "scalawags" (Texans who supported the Union against the South) as well as some "carpetbaggers" (Northerners who moved to the South after the war hoping to exploit the volatile situation). Contrary to popular belief, carpetbaggers held a minority of public offices in the state and probably served as scapegoats for the South's Reconstruction problems. Delegates fought among themselves, some wanting to divide Texas into three separate states, others arguing that all laws passed during the Confederacy lacked a legal foundation, and radicals demanding civil rights for blacks, which outraged conservative Texans. The convention finally recessed without drafting a new constitution.

Before convention delegates met again in December of 1868, President Johnson was on the verge of impeachment and lost the 1868 election. Popular Republican presidential nominee Ulysses S. Grant defeated Andrew Johnson, whose Southern appeasement program had alienated both Congress and the public. Republicans, believing that Johnson wanted to sabotage their Reconstruction program, had brought impeachment charges in early 1868. The House eventually impeached Johnson by a vote of 126 to 47, but the Senate fell one vote short of the necessary two-thirds, and he remained in office.

Continued turmoil in Texas led moderates to gain control of the state convention, which resulted in the passing of a new constitution that increased the governor's power, provided educational funds for children, and gave all male citizens the right to vote, regardless of race or color. Moderate Democrats and Republicans nominated A. J. Hamilton for governor, and the radicals chose Edmund J. Davis, a brigadier-general in the Union army who had returned to Texas after the war. Davis won the election by a small margin, which brought charges of fraud from both President Grant and prominent Texans. Governor Pease, meanwhile, resigned in protest over military intervention in the state's affairs.

The Davis administration remains one of the most divisive in Texas history. A Republican-dominated legislature passed acts that many politicians and voters opposed. The creation of a state militia, a state police force, and the ability to declare martial law gave the governor immense power. He appointed thousands of government employees, created a state-subsidized press—which came under heavy fire from opponents—and even controlled the voter registration system. Railroad legislation also raised eyebrows. Post-revisionists have tried to vindicate Davis, whose political clout enabled him to suppress Ku Klux Klan activity, promote a more equitable tax burden, and establish a centralized free public school system supported by taxes that placed the state far ahead of its time.

Public opinion, however, turned against the Davis administration. In 1871, representatives from ninety-four counties met to protest the government's wasteful spending program and its violation of constitutional laws. When the legislature reconvened, Democrats again gained state control and repealed many of the laws and programs of the Davis administration. In 1873, Davis ran against Richard Coke for governor but lost the election by a landslide, although some cried bribery and intimidation. Davis refused to vacate office, threatening to use the state police force, and sent an appeal to President Grant who advised him to be prudent and step down. He still refused until another letter arrived from the attorney general of the U.S.

The Coke administration removed Republicans from office and rewrote the state constitution to eliminate centralized government and reduce the power of courts, judges, and the governor. It also abolished a centralized school system and left education up to local governments. Coke later won the 1876 state election by a vote of three to one.

Thus, the turbulent period of Reconstruction ended in Texas, which remained under Democratic control for decades. Because of the state's size, it's hard to make any generalizations about this unstable period. Loyalties differed depending on climate, topography, and sectional jealousies. Planters in the eastern and southeastern areas who grew cotton depended on the plantation system, while those in western frontier settlements worried about Indian depredations. Strangely enough, this post-Reconstruction age has been romanticized by endless novels and Hollywood westerns—an age of desperadoes, wild Indians, and cowboy cattle drives across the plains that helped perpetuate the richness of Texas folklore.

Chapter IX

Cowboys, Comanches, and Crooks

"Other states were carved or born. Texas grew from hide and horn."
—Bret Harte

The Spanish brought cattle to Mexico in the 16th century. They spread across the country, mixing with other wild stock, and finally crossed the Rio Grande into the U.S. When English-speaking settlers came to Texas in the early 1820s, they found wild cattle everywhere—the ancestors of Texas' famed longhorns. Thousands soon roamed the colony. By the time the Republic of Texas became a state in 1846, large-boned longhorns with swayed backs and lyre-shaped horns had multiplied into the millions.

THE BEEF BONANZA

After the war between Mexico and the U.S., drovers began to sell longhorns to Indianola, Mobile, New Orleans, and other coast towns for meat. Some went to California and Rocky Mountain mining camps during the gold rushes. Frontier military posts also needed supplies. Some cowmen took routes over hot deserts and Indian territory. But outbreaks of "Texas fever" (a cattle disease caused by ticks) hit Missouri and Kansas after the Civil War because of infected Texas cattle. Farmers and stockmen stopped drovers at the borders, and both states passed laws barring all Texan cattle to protect their own herds. Despite the Texas fever epidemic, this era saw the start of large ranchers such as Richard King and Mifflin Kenedy, who joined to establish the King Ranch, now one of the world's largest. Other later cattle barons, such as "Shanghai" Pierce, George Webb Slaughter, and Charles Goodnight, also began herds.

The Civil War, quarantine laws, and Comanche-Kiowa attacks temporarily halted cattle drives. President Lincoln forbade any trade with the South during the war. The Confederate states needed supplies for their army, but that also ended after 1863 when the Union gained control of the Mississippi River, cutting off traffic to New Orleans. A few Texan blockade runners managed to elude federal gunboats and crossed the Mississippi below Vicksburg to make big profits supplying Southern commissary depots. Others trafficked with the North for federal gold. Most male Texans joined the army, leaving wives and children to tend crops and animals, which resulted in unbranded and neglected herds that ran wild. Indians, rustlers, and army deserters also stole countless cattle during this period. Some Confederate deserters even took herds to Mexico.

It's fascinating how the Civil War influenced the Texas cattle kingdom that ran between 1865 and late 1880s. While Texas cattle increased in number during the raging conflict, those in the North decreased as Union armies exhausted meat supplies. In addition, Kansas, Iowa, and Minnesota pioneers switched from cattle to farming in favor of cheaper and faster-growing crops. The war also spurred the spread of railroads as Congress made enormous land grants and subsidies.

Before long, millions of Texas longhorns roamed mostly unbranded, without a way to market and make a profit off them. Many were killed for hides, bones, and tallow. One person remarked that "a man's poverty was estimated by the number of cattle he possessed." Some beef went to frontier army posts and to Indian reservations, but for the most part, Texas remained cow poor because there wasn't a way to ship them east. A cow worth $5 or $6 in Texas fetched ten times as much in the North. Rustlers stampeded herds and murdered drovers who reached southeastern Kansas and southwestern Missouri. Crooked operators shipped Texas cattle to New Orleans and Havana, Cuba, cleaning up off shady deals.

Texas needed a way to market millions of cattle to Northerners over known trails. The Chisholm Trail took its name from half-breed Indian trader Jesse Chisholm and stretched from San Antonio to Abilene, Kansas, a distance of about eight hundred miles. Other prongs fed into this northbound trail, such as the Goodnight-Living Trail and the Western Trail that led to Dodge City. Sections overlapped with the old Shawnee Trail. In time, many cowpunchers referred to all these routes as the Chisholm Trail.

A clever promoter and livestock dealer, Joseph G. McCoy saw the need for a railhead where drovers could sell their stock. He chose the tent town of Abilene, Kansas, because of its location at the northern end of the

Chapter IX: Cowboys, Comanches, and Crooks

Painting entitled "The Approaching Herd"

Chisholm Trail and its abundant grass and water, then marketed it through circulars, newspapers, and plenty of promotion. He later wrote: "Abilene in 1867 was a very small, dead place, consisting of about one dozen log huts, low, small, rude affairs, four-fifths of which were covered with dirt for roofing; indeed, but one shingle roof could be seen in the whole city. The business of the burg was conducted in two small rooms, mere log huts, and of course the inevitable saloon, also in a log hut, was to be found."

McCoy faced tough resistance from the railroads at first, but he persisted and finally got the small Hannibal and St. Joe Railroad interested. This helped start the movement to Northern markets which mushroomed almost overnight. He built shipping pens, a livery stable, barns, and a three-story hotel. The center prospered for awhile, reaching a peak of 600,000 head of cattle in 1871, before eastern shipping points moved to other wild and wooly trail towns such as Ellsworth and Dodge City, Kansas.

Texas cattle drives flourished during the next couple decades, although they suffered some setbacks such as a cholera epidemic, farmer opposition, and the Panic of 1873, when banks tightened moneylending. The state, well-suited for cattle because of its climate and open ranges, allowed free grazing from the Gulf to the Red River. It's estimated that about 35,000 cowboys worked the cattle trail during this period, earning between $15

A Texas cowboy

and $40 a month. Some were drifters, others sought work after the Civil War, and the rest just liked adventure and the outdoor life.

Cowboys faced many hardships, including Indian attacks, stampedes, ice storms, flooded rivers, guerrilla gangs, angry farmers, and disease. One trail driver recalled that "the country was one vast stretch of rich land, no timber except on creeks or rivers … There were all sizes of herds, from five hundred to twenty-five hundred cattle in a drove, usually seven or eight men to the small herds and twelve to fifteen men with large herds." A sudden or unfamiliar sound might spook high-strung longhorns and cause a stampede. They ran off bluffs and into gullies, breaking legs and killing one another. Thirsty longhorns went crazy over the smell of water and could drown in swollen rivers and creeks. They also froze and starved during winter blizzards. All this could exhaust cowpunchers. One grumbled, "Have not got the Blues but am in Hell of a fix … My back is Blistered badly … Flies was worse than I ever saw them … One man down with Boils & one with Ague … Found a human skeleton on the Prairie to day."

The rise of railroads eventually ended cattle drives in Texas, along with a revolutionary frontier invention—barbed wire. Scarcity of rocks and timber in open country made it difficult to fence in land. Smooth wire had been used on the prairies, but it contracted in cold weather, expanded in hot weather, and cost too much. Studies by the Department of Agriculture at that time found its use would cost farmers twice as much as they'd make from crops. They even concluded that the cost to fence in ranches would equal the national debt and value of all farm animals in the country. So the fence question became a burning issue throughout the state.

During the 1870s, ranchers began to fence in their lands with barbed wire, although many disliked it at first because horses and cattle cut themselves. The practice also denied trail drivers rights to grass and water holes. One big outfit strung six hundred miles of barbed wire around its land. Some cattle barons leased vast sections of land from the government for pennies an acre, and then fenced in areas of public domain in order to squeeze out settlers and small operators. The advent of barbed-wire fencing in Texas hindered mail delivery, cut off public roads, and stopped people on horseback from getting to school or church.

Clashes flared between fencers and free-grazers, leading to a fence-cutting range war in the 1880s when saboteurs burned pastures, emptied water tanks, and drove off animals. Cowmen who didn't own land and relied on free ranges also suffered losses. The governor called a special session of the legislature in 1884 that made fence cutting a felony and required ranchers who strung barbed wire across public roads to provide a gate every three miles. Damages during the range war ran into the millions, and tax income slumped around thirty million in Texas. Settlers also stayed away and some small farmers even left the state.

Barbed wire also helped fuel another kind of range war in Texas—one between cattlemen and sheep herders. By 1886 around 4,750,000 sheep grazed in the state. Both the background and lifestyles of cowboys and sheep herders differed. Most herders were older men who understood wool production, while the younger rowdy cowboys resented these intruders. Ranchers argued that cattle couldn't share the same land as sheep because "everything in front of a sheep is eaten, and everything behind is killed." Sheep eat grass close to the ground and trample it because they range close together. Violence erupted on the great plains. Texas law prevented sheep from grazing on someone else's property without their permission—which cattlemen refused to give—yet sheep herders continued to graze flocks on these lands. In retaliation, cattlemen covered their faces with cloth sacks and struck herder camps during the night. These gunnysackers beat and even murdered wool growers and killed thousands of sheep. Fences were cut, homes burned, and wagons destroyed. Damage ran into the millions before these two factions decided to bury the hatchet and share the range.

Depiction of a cattle raid on the Texas border, 1874

Yet barbed-wire fencing aided Texas cowmen and farmers in many ways. It reduced the number of strays and stolen animals. Fenced cows became tamer and less prone to stampede. Closing trails reduced the spread of disease, and controlled breeding improved blood stock. Farmers also benefited because cattle on the trail trampled crops and ate grass leaving farmland stripped. Barbed wire helped homesteader settlement, land and farm improvements, and led to western expansion and the growth of prosperous cities.

During this exciting period, millions of cattle walked to market from Texas, surviving droughts, rustlers, and Comanche-Kiowa attacks. The long drives, however, ended by the late 1880s. Reasons for this dramatic shift included barbed-wire fence, farmers settling in Kansas and adjacent states, quarantine laws, and railroad expansion that enabled Texans to ship cattle directly to Chicago instead of through Kansas. Northern prices also fell during this era because of overstocks. By 1900, the demand for Texas cattle once again increased with even greater profits.

The age of cattle drives became an entrenched part of U.S. growth.

Powerful packing houses such as Swift and Armour mass produced and controlled beef, using refrigerated freight cars to transport it. In 1892 *Scribner's Magazine* mused that "the life that surrounded [the cattle trails] could not endure. The homes of thousands of settlers have pre-emptied the grazing grounds. Railroads are ten times more numerous than were the trails, and like the cavalier, the troubadour, the Puritan, and the 'Forty-Niner,' the cowboy and his attendant life have become figures in history."

LORDS OF THE SOUTH PLAINS

Indian raids reached an all-time high on the Texas frontier after the Civil War, causing many settlers to abandon homes or protect themselves by "forting up" together behind stockades. Renegade bands attacked south of the Red River during the "light of the moon," stealing horses and cattle, scalping farmers, and burning homes. Comanches and other hostile tribes ruled the vast mesaland of the South High Plains called the Llano Estacado as ancestral hunting grounds, sometimes marauding as far south as Durango, Mexico. Many called this stamping ground the Great Comanche War Trail. T. R. Fehrenback says in *Comanche* that "this secondary western front was as tragic as the secession holocaust. White-Amerindian conflict took on deeper and bloodier dimensions; a new generation was brutalized; and both whites and Amerindians suffered terribly from a long attrition."

A number of factors helped defeat the Texas Plains Indians. With the expansion of railroads, miners, settlers and cattlemen continued to migrate West. The nomadic Indians lacked central leadership, the ability to adapt, and clung to intertribal rivalries. They also failed to grasp the extent of U.S. military power. Three key factors finally ended their control of the Texas Panhandle and surrounding region: the U.S. regular army, the Texas Rangers, and extermination of the enormous buffalo herds.

U.S. REGULAR ARMY

Even though the army began building a line of military forts in the late 1860s that ran from the Rio Grande to the Red River—around six hundred miles—it took years to complete these defenses. Timber was scarce and often freighted hundreds of miles. Roofs leaked and dust fell from the ceilings. Fleas, centipedes, and scorpions infested crowded quarters. Winter winds and summer heat made life hard for soldiers.

A Congressional bill created a Peace Commission to tackle the Indian problem. Representatives traveled to Medicine Lodge Creek in Kansas to forge a lasting treaty with tribes of the region, hoping to get Indians off the range so westward expansion could continue. This treaty failed like previous ones because neither side honored its articles. Indian depredations continued on the Texas plains. Abuses flourished. Traders who wanted to sell guns and ammunition urged Indians to raid on the frontier. Bootleggers traded cheap whiskey for valuable buffalo robes. Thieves made profits from thousands of stolen horses, some even committing crimes disguised as Indians.

In 1869 Congress finally passed the Indian Appropriation Act which authorized President Grant to appoint a board to supervise Indian affairs. This resulted in the Quaker Policy to reduce corruption among politicians and agents of reservations through the appointment of peace-seeking Quakers, although Grant still filled many agency posts with military officers. Restless Indians slipped away from reservations to raid settlers before returning to protected lands. Few wanted to farm or send their children to school. Others sought guns and ammunition to hunt buffalo meat and asked for the removal of reservation boundary lines. General Sheridan finally concluded that "the whole Indian management is a notorious fraud."

Frontier conditions grew frantic. Even with federal troops on Texas soil, Indians could easily slip through gaps between forts, sometimes up to eighty-five miles apart. The cries of Texans finally reached Washington. Inspector General Randolph Marcy and General Sherman finally went on a border tour between San Antonio and the Kansas Pacific Railroad in 1871. They passed one burned out fort and ranch after another. Marcy wrote in his journal: "This rich and beautiful section does not contain today so many white people as it did when I visited it eighteen years ago, and if the Indian marauders are not punished, the whole country seems to be in a fair way of becoming totally depopulated."

The column reached Fort Richardson that night after passing along Salt Creek Prairie and barely missed a band of 150 Comanche Indians who later massacred a corn train of teamsters, leaving one man hung upside down and burned alive. The outraged Sherman called for immediate action. Comanche Chief Santana was arrested and found guilty of murder, but went free after claiming he could prevent Indian raids in the future. He later served more time and committed suicide.

After the capture of Santana, the Kiowa and Comanche went back on the warpath. The Indian Bureau arranged several Indian trips to Washington, hoping to impress tribes with a show of power, while the army continued to send forces after hostile Comanches. Things quieted down for a while. But when hidemen ravaged buffalo herds in Kansas, the herds moved south of the Platte River in Comanche territory into the Texas Panhandle—off limits because of the Medicine Creek Treaty. Stung by violations and agitated by chiefs Quanah Parker and Isatai (Little Wolf), the Comanches, Kiowas, and several other tribes called a war council. They first planned to attack Tonkawas, scouts and guides for the army, but then chose the buffalo trading post Adobe Walls in the Texas Panhandle, hoping to scalp sleeping hunters and freighters. Their plan backfired in June 1874. Traders and hidemen had been up repairing the roof of a saloon and fought off the siege from three buildings with powerful Sharpe buffalo rifles. They barricaded doors and windows with sacks of grain and packing crates, shooting from behind the mud chinking. Help finally arrived from other buffalo hunters who beat back the Indians.

The Adobe Walls fight turned the tide against marauding Indians. Buffalo hunters vacated the post with supplies and thousands of hides, moving southward to shipping points such as Fort Griffin and later Fort Worth. Some quit buffalo hunting. The Indians, who later returned and burned the post, suffered a worse fate: U.S. army intervention.

Open warfare now existed. General Sherman formed five commands that converged near the Red River with orders to crush all Indian resistance, the largest military movement ever undertaken on the Southern Plains. Ronald S. Mackenzie, called by General Grant "the most promising young officer in the army," commanded the successful operation. Mackenzie, who had earlier sought Quanah's raiders on the Texas border, found himself after the elusive chief once again. He needed to find the Indian encampment before winter set in. Fortunately, scouts located the hidden villages at Palo Duro Canyon, around a thousand feet deep and difficult to descend. Indians scattered. Mackenzie burned everything: lodges, food supplies, guns. He also gave orders to shoot most of the captured mules and horses.

The Battle of Palo Duro Canyon crippled Indian power in the Panhandle, mainly because in the winter months they were left without horses or supplies. Over a dozen other skirmishes followed as the army relentlessly tracked down remaining hostile parties. In the spring of 1875, the renegades finally surrendered, ending the moonlight raids that had horrified settlers for decades. Chief Quanah Parker brought the remaining Comanches to Fort Sill and then became a celebrity, even riding down Pennsylvania Avenue during the second inaugural of President Theodore Roosevelt.

Apache resistance still remained in the far west area of Texas under

Chief Victorio, who raided from both sides of the Rio Grande. A joint Mexican-American force swept through his remote hiding places in Mexico and in 1880 trapped Victorio in the Tres Castillos Mountains. For the next decade, minor clashes still occurred, but the Indian wars had ended.

The Texas Devils (Los Diablos Tejanos)

During the first years of American settlement in Texas, Stephen F. Austin needed a force to protect settlers from Mexican robbers and nomadic Indians. These men became known as Rangers because they could be "ranged" anywhere a need existed on the Texas plains. Austin called a conference that asked for twenty to thirty Rangers. Landowners were asked to serve or provide a substitute one month for every half league of land they owned (a league is about three miles). It wasn't until 1835, however, that the Texas Rangers became officially organized.

Unlike army troops, they chose their own leaders, attire, horses—and scoffed at military order. Their unconventional garb turned eyes. As one recruit wrote: "Most of them were dressed in skins, some wearing parts of buffalo robes, deer skins and bear skins, and some entirely naked to the waist, but having heavy leggings and necessary breech-clouts. All were well armed and well mounted."

In order to outsmart the Indians, Rangers learned to think and act like them—which meant surprise attacks, no quarter in battle, and expert horsemanship. Horses had enabled Comanches to defeat the Spanish and Mexicans, terrorize Texas settlers, and play cat and mouse with the U.S. military for over a century. General Marcy called their equestrian feats

Engraving of Texas Rangers fighting Indians

"truly astonishing." Painter-traveler George Catlin also called the Comanches "extraordinary," and questioned whether "any people in the world can surpass them." Rangers needed an edge over warriors on the warpath. Their single-barrel, muzzle-loading rifles were too long, too heavy, and needed reloading after one shot. Colt's Paterson five-shooter changed all that. (Colt was granted a patent for a "revolving gun" in 1836. In 1847 Texas Rangers ordered one thousand revolvers to use in the Mexican-American War.) As the Texas saying went: "God made some men big and some men small, but Col. Sam Colt made them equal all." This repeating firearm allowed Rangers to shoot at close range, which shocked the Comanches. After one battle, a chief reputedly said: "I will never again fight Jack Hayes, whose men have a shot for every finger on the hand."

The illustrious yet scarred history of the Texas Rangers hasn't affected the romantic Wild West notions of writers and film heroes such as the Lone Ranger. In real life, the army disliked their ruthless, cold-blooded tactics, but they were efficient and got the job done. Before the Civil War, Rangers such as Jack Hayes, Ben McCulloch, William A. "Big Foot" Wallace, and Samuel H. Walker not only tracked down renegade Indians, but joined the abortive Santa Fe and Mier Expeditions. They also served during the Mexican War as scouts and spies, leading civilians to call them *los Diablo Tejanos*.

When the Civil War broke out, Rangers filled gaps on the frontier left by troops, patrolling from the Red River to the Rio Grande. During the Reconstruction era, Ranger activity against Indian raids on the frontier continued. Sometimes they lost fights, but they patrolled the plains, gradually becoming more involved in law after their services became legal. During this later period, Rangers defused the Sutton-Taylor Feud and suppressed riots such as the El Paso Salt War of 1877, the Laredo Election Riot of 1886, and the Rio Grande City Riot of 1886. They also caught outlaws.

Although the U.S. Army and Texas Rangers made crucial contributions to end the Indian threat to Texas settlement, one other factor made this long-term success possible—destruction of the vast buffalo herds.

BUFFALO ON THE BORDER

As early as the 16th century, Cabeza de Vaca called Texas buffalo "wild cows." Coronado's later expedition also saw herds of these shaggy-haired, humped animals, possibly in the Texas Panhandle. So did other Spanish explorers. Franciscan monks found buffalo around Monterey and Northern Mexico. By the 19th century, vast herds roamed along the Southern

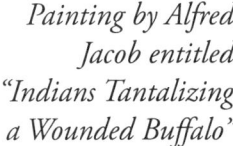

Painting by Alfred Jacob entitled "Indians Tantalizing a Wounded Buffalo"

Plains. Witnesses reported one herd fifty miles long and twenty-five miles wide in 1871, while others said it sometimes took days for a herd to pass. They were compared to "fish in the sea," "the locusts of Egypt," and "in numbers—numberless."

Greedy hunters quickly reduced these figures. By 1880 only a few hundred buffalo remained on the Texas plains. The nomadic Indians depended on these animals for their existence and grew alarmed at the mindless slaughter. Unlike hide hunters, the Indians used nearly every part of the buffalo for food, shelter, and clothing. The hides provided robes, moccasins, and lodge coverings, the flesh provided food, ribs provided runners for small sleds, hoofs provided glue, and sinews provided

thread and bow strings. Even the dried chips (droppings) of buffalo were used to cook food. Indians also bartered the buffalo products with traders for sugar, coffee, and blankets. With the end of the buffalo came the end of the Indian tribes.

    Although use of Indian hunting grounds lessened during the Civil War, this changed in the 1870s when the demand for buffalo hides to make leather products rose. Buffalo profits soared at first. The animals didn't cost anything to raise, and hundreds could be shot in a few hours or days. Hides fetched $3.50 each in Dodge City, but within a couple years, their value dropped to around $1.00. Tons of meat worth only pennies a pound rotted on the prairie. Some hunters just took buffalo horns. Railroads offered hunting excursions in which the rich shot buffalo from the comfort of cars for fun or as trophies. Men who sold hides swarmed over the buffalo range with high-powered firearms. Buffalo Bill Cody bagged 4,280 in an eighteen-month period for railroad construction crews to eat. The slaughter continued until the great herds vanished forever.

When the buffalo disappeared, homesteaders and some Indians collected their white bones which covered the prairies, grinding them up for phosphorous fertilizer and sugar refining. Between 1872 and 1874, railroads transported more than thirty million pounds, which brought up to ten dollars a ton at market. Some piles stood eight or ten feet high and half a mile long at rail stations. Horns and hoofs were also made into buttons, combs, and glue. By 1880 that market was also exhausted.

After the extinction of buffalo on the Southwest plains, Indian tribes accepted government help and grew more tolerant of reservations. This opened the way for Western expansion and the rapid growth of farming, railroads, and the Texas cattle kingdom. By 1878 outposts built to ward off Indians after the Mexican War stood abandoned. Texas's population began to explode. In 1875 only 150,000 people lived in West Texas. This increased to over 550,000 by 1890.

WILD WEST OUTLAWS

Many Texans returned home broke after the Civil War. They couldn't find work and so became cattle rustlers, bushwackers, and gunslingers. In 1874 the U.S. government formed the Frontier Battalion, which guarded Texas from the Red River to the Nueces River. Rangers had their hands full with criminals who were hard to track over hundreds of miles. Fugitives also fled to Mexico. Jesse and Frank James hooked up with William Quantrill in east Texas. The Younger brothers and Belle Star hung out in the Dallas area, Billy the Kid in Old Tascosa, and cattle town Fort Worth was home to Butch Cassidy and Sundance Kid. The two most infamous Texas bandits? Probably Sam Bass and John Wesley Hardin.

Illiterate Sam Bass robbed stagecoaches, trains, and banks. His most famous train holdup in 1877 looted $60,000 (worth around two million today) for the gang in new twenty-dollar gold pieces from a Wells Fargo Express car in Nebraska. After squandering his cut, Bass continued to rob trains in the Dallas area and finally a bank at Round Rock, where Rangers mortally wounded this desperado. His last words were, "The world is bobbing around."

Bad man John Wesley Hardin (named after the founder of the

Methodist Church's John Wesley) reputedly killed dozens of men. He served seventeen years in prison, studied law, and was admitted to the Texas bar after his release. While in prison, he wrote an autobiography in which he preached: "If you wish to be successful in life, be temperate and control your passions; if you don't ruin and death is the inevitable result." But fate finally caught up with the hated Hardin. On August 22, 1895, he was shot in the back by a constable while playing dice in an El Paso saloon. The justice of the peace remarked, "Had he been shot from in front I would have called it excellent marksmanship. As he was shot from behind, I have to call it excellent judgment."

Outlaws such as Bass and Hardin became legends of the rugged West. Tired of corrupt bankers and railroad moguls who charged inflated rates, some misguided Texans defended these hooligans. Women sent Hardin gifts in prison. J. Lee Butts says in *Texas Bad Boys*: "Americans have always harbored an uncommon degree of affection for their darker natured outlaw cousins of the nineteenth century. The degree of interest and respect we tend to heap on thieves, reprobates, degenerates, pimps, gunmen, and sharks ... borders on the downright loopy."

Chapter X

The New Gospel of Political Salvation

"Enforce the laws, show no quarter to any man who will practice frauds on the people by inflated, fictitious securities. Let capital know that in Texas a written obligation means what it says, and that all public securities will be strictly scrutinized by a state jealous of her reputation for honesty in all things."

—James Stephen Hogg

Railroads revolutionized American travel in the 19th century—but Texas got off to a slow start. Although the Republic chartered several lines, squabbling and money shortages prevented any from being built. Foreign investors avoided speculation in a country with one person per square mile and only three real centers: San Antonio, Goliad, and Nacogdoches. Steamers later operated on waterways, but mud flats, sand bogs, and swollen streams made it hard to reach interior towns. Crooked, rutted roads, and the "black waxy prairies" impaired wagons. Streams lacked bridges. Mules and oxen still transported most goods. Uncomfortable, expensive stagecoaches traveled around ten miles an hour. Jefferson Davis, secretary of war, brought camels to Texas in the 1850s in an attempt to relieve conditions, but the Civil War and the army's indifference ended this curious experiment.

Before the Civil War, fewer than a dozen small railroads operated in the state, mostly near the Houston area. Texas had only 307 miles of track. Railroad growth ceased during the war. Hard times afterwards limited funds to repair existing lines and finance new ones. When the Transcon-

Early photo of the Texas and Pacific Railroad

tinental Railroad opened in 1869, Texas still had less than five hundred miles of track. Farmers who raised cotton, grain, and hides transported freight by road on wagons and ox carts to shipping ports, where barges and steamboats carried goods to coastal centers such as Galveston and Corpus Christi. Fees were high—around $1.00 per one hundred pounds per one hundred miles, which could absorb half a crop's value. Farmers and merchants alike saw the need for a faster, cheaper, and more dependable means of transportation to market goods.

Texas was dirt poor. But dirt saved the day with a hundred million acres of public lands. The state offered land grants—sixteen sections (10,240 acres) for each mile of track—around 32,150,000 acres before the act was repealed in 1882. Towns also enticed railroad companies. They gave right-of-way through counties, built depots, offered tax breaks, and even bribed companies with cash. For example, the city of Marshall offered the Texas Pacific Railroad several hundred thousand dollars in

Cotton bales on Galveston wharf during Progressive period

county bonds and 66 acres of land for depots and shops. Towns that resisted stagnated because the railroad line bypassed them. When the prosperous river port of Jefferson refused to give incentives, the railroad went through Marshall, causing Jefferson's rapid decline. Other places, such as Washington-on-the-Brazos, once the capital of Texas, became ghost towns. On the other hand, thriving cities such as Houston, Dallas, and Fort Worth owed their fast growth to the railroad, which continued to expand because of huge profits. By 1900 nearly ten thousand miles of track crisscrossed the state.

Two men monopolized railroad expansion in the state. Collis P. Huntington, the country's leading railroad builder, controlled the enormous Central Pacific-Southern Pacific system along with Leland Stanford, each expanding their empire by buying small lines. In addition, Eastern mogul Jay Gould, who wanted control of Missouri, Kansas, and Texas rails, ran the Missouri Pacific Lines whose holdings included a handful of smaller Texas railroads, about one-third of the state's mileage, and connected with the National Mexico Railroad which went to Mexico City. When Gould spread into the West, Huntington huffed, "Their people have gone in our bailiwick, and they don't belong there." But the two men signed an agreement in 1882 that fixed rates, enabling their lines to jointly use the Sierra Blanca-El Paso line, giving them control of most Texas railroads.

One of the most colorful characters in Texas history became famous because of a railroad. Saloonkeeper Judge Roy Bean got involved with the Southern Pacific and the Galveston, Harrisburg, and San Antonio Railroad in Dead Man's Canyon. Rowdy crews and tent towns filled with saloons, gambling dens, and dance-hall girls led to drinking and shootings. County commissioners made Bean justice of the peace for Pecos County. He held court in the construction camp of Vinegaroon which sat on a rocky hill above the blasting of a tunnel. After the railroad's completion, Bean hung a sign over the front of his bar that read "Law West of the Pecos" and "Justice of the Peace." He also organized the famous Fitzsimmons-Maher boxing match on a sandbar in the Rio Grande River because the state outlawed boxing.

Railroads, of course, brought many benefits to the state, employing more workers than any other industry in the Southwest. They encouraged immigration and land settlement, crop growth, and increased taxable land, as well as connecting the state with outer regions of the country. Property values increased from around $51,000,000 in 1850 to $886,000,000 in 1890. Thousands of laborers, skilled and unskilled, found work. Steam-powered locomotives began to burn coal instead of wood. This led to mining cheap, low-quality fossil fuel in towns such as Coalville and Thurber, west of Fort Worth—around two million tons in the 1890s. The Texas and Pacific Railroad alone used 360,000 tons of coal a year. Quarries mined granite, salt, limestone, and copper, which were shipped by railroads, as well as iron from several smelting factories. Repair shops along routes not only caused old towns to grow but also new ones to sprout up.

The east Texas lumber industry also owed its success to railroads. As early as 1828, Stephen F. Austin saw the potential of pine timber. Transportation to distant markets became the chief problem. Most early sawmills were built along rivers near the Gulf Coast. Others floated the logs on rafts down east Texas rivers to big mills in cities such as Beaumont and Houston. After mills made the logs into lumber, boats and steamboats took the lumber to coastal towns. But these rivers were unreliable and hazardous sources of travel. Loggers needed a complex network of railroads that made the isolated east Texas lumber industry reachable. John Henry Kirby, known as "prince of the pines," eventually set up the Kirby Lumber Company, the largest in the world, and built the G.B.&K.C. railroad to connect his many properties. Dozens of other small company-owned rails also pierced the piney forests, some getting charters to operate passenger service and even buying timberland. By 1910 around 625 lumber mills dotted the state.

Railroads and the lumber industry also led to the rise of unions in Texas. Few of these existed before the 1870s. Isolated and uneducated farm workers lacked knowledge of such associations and newspapers rarely printed articles about them. The progressive Screwman's Benevolent Association (SBA) of Galveston (a trade union whose members stored and packed cotton bales in the holds of ships) not only provided sick and death benefits to members but also adopted a medical plan. When Norris Wright Cuney organized the Black Longshoremen's Benevolent Association, SBA members complained that unskilled workers took the place of qualified ones and walked out. The strike failed. Members returned to work and blacks continued at the trade. However, the 1910 invention of the high-density cotton compress ended the screwmen's craft and led to the union's demise.

Over one hundred strikes occurred in Texas as the state shifted from an agricultural to an industrial economy. Strikers included workers in the building trades, railroads, longshoremen, and even discontented cowboys. For example, organized labor groups held a strike while building the new statehouse because they resented the use of convicts and foreign laborers as granite cutters. Jay Gould's Texas and Pacific Railroad also suffered a strike because of irregular paydays and substandard salaries—less than $500 a year for nearly 50 percent of employees. When the governor ignored the protestors' grievances, the Knights of Labor called a strike. Other walkouts followed throughout the Southwest. Ten thousand railroad workers and ninety thousand workers in the lumber industry became unemployed. Mills and factories closed. Perishables rotted on tracks. Prices soared for foods. The governor finally called out the militia and Texas Rangers to restore order, which weakened the Knights of Labor and other unions.

KING COTTON—CASH CROP

The railroads also enabled commercial farming to flourish—especially cotton, which soon became more profitable than cattle. Frontier settlers found the land hospitable to this agricultural crop, which depleted the soil less than staples such as corn and wheat, seldom failed, and fetched more money at market. During the pre-railroad Civil War, cotton sales to European markets helped Texans buy goods, medicine, and munitions. Thereafter, it became a cash crop for farmers, around 150,000 bales a year by 1870.

As railroads spread and the frontier in west Texas vanished, farmers poured into the area from the South and Europe. Railroad companies urged settlement in brochures and even ran trains to select sites, hoping to increase the number of settlers reliant upon the railroads. "Go to Texas" ads appeared throughout the country. One New Orleans newspaper wrote in 1886 that "ranchmen have just enough time to move their cattle out and prevent their tails being chopped off by the advancing hoe." King cotton tenaciously took hold. Nearly half of all farmland in the state grew it, which enabled rapid town and industrial growth. The yearly value of cotton reached $100,000,000 by the century's end. (Texas remains the largest cotton-producing state with 5.4 million acres in 2010.) Cottonseed also became profitable.

But growing cotton, like other agricultural products, caused many hardships. One farmer wrote to a cousin: "This has been a season with me. My mind has been stretched to its utmost tension to brave the story that we little thought would come over the country this time last year. The destroying of the crops, the long siege of the yellow fever, the low price of cotton, and other ills I have had to keep my mind steadily fixed not to break or loose [sic] credit." Cash-strapped farmers began to evolve methods for getting the most out of their harvest. Some started to use windmills for irrigation. Others built terraces or ridges to catch rainfall. Plowing also helped loosen dirt for better absorption. Machines such as steam-powered tractors later gave farmers more leisure time, but commercial farming was expensive and forced owners to run into debt. It also led to overproduction and the fall of cotton prices—from 16.5 cents a pound in 1869 to 5.7 cents a pound in 1898. Depressed cotton prices meant trouble for farmers and merchants alike because bankers foreclosed on land.

Unlike crop prices, the Panic of 1873 had led farmers to blame suppliers, middlemen, and speculators for their problems. Many investors and small farmers lost their shirts in such an unstable economic climate. Merchants charged high interest rates because they needed to pay wholesalers. Lending money to small farmers also involved high risks because of uncertain crops, which depended on weather and market values. In 1878 an east Texan wrote: "Money is hardly to be had, at all, outside of the banks. And there the interest is ruinous. I know of nobody making money in our country." And in 1893 insects called boll weevils ruined 90 percent of the cotton crop in southern Texas.

By the late 19th century, around half of all farmers were either tenant or sharecroppers. Tenant farmers rented the land on which they lived and farmed, but seldom made enough to purchase the property. Sharecroppers paid rent with a share of crops. Few broke even because they bought goods on credit from landlords and often owed more than they earned at season's end.

LABOR AND THE LAND SHARKS

Since the 1870s, the conservative Republican Party tended to dominate Texas politics because of Anglo influence and sore memories of the radical Republican Reconstruction period. The demonetizing of silver in 1873 and the Specie Resumption Act in 1875 led to a reduced money supply, especially in the South, already impoverished from the Civil War. Wheat fell from $1.00 a bushel in 1870 to $.60 a bushel in the 1890s. Cattle prices also plummeted. Land sold for several dollars an acre. Yet the number of farms in Texas increased from around 61,000 in 1870 to over 350,000 in 1900.

After the Civil War, weary farmers formed organizations such as the Grange, the Greenbackers, and the Farmers' Alliance to improve conditions and control railroad abuses. The later People's Party adopted many platforms from these organizations. Yet even with more bank credit, rail-

Chapter X: The New Gospel of Political Salvation

Windmill on a south Texas farm

road regulation, and reduced taxes, the uneducated, small grower fought a losing battle against progress. Northerners dealt with this struggle by moving to industrialized cities. In Texas, big ranches continued to buy up land and squeeze out sharecroppers and the small landowners, helped along by outside "big business" and new, expensive machinery. Farmers couldn't compete with Northern goods as cotton prices continued to tumble. Discontent finally led many to join socialist and radical organizations. These people wanted to set things straight for "the industrialized millions."

The Grange

The National Grange or Patrons of Husbandry began after the Civil War in 1867. Texas boasted a membership of 45,000 by the late 1870s. Grange lodges tried to reduce the costs of farm goods by running 150 cooperative stores that bought in bulk and sold goods to farmers at bulk prices. They also protested unfair railroad practices such as charging more for short hauls than long ones. (Short hauls involved less competition than longer ones and supposedly showed a smaller profit.) Railroads also gave free passes and rebates to shippers and politicians which caused more friction. Grange pressure led the legislature to pass an act in 1879 that provided uniform rates, but it was hard to enforce. Problems arose when the National Grange extended credit to cooperatives that bought goods on credit from wholesalers. Droughts during the mid-1880s—which caused many bankruptcies—and weak managerial skills among leaders caused the system to crumble. By 1890 only five thousand members remained.

The Greenbackers

Greenback clubs wanted more money circulated in the form of greenbacks (paper money) as legal tender for debts, which they believed would cause farm prices to rise. These dissident small farmers and ranchers, who also sought better schools, an income tax, and railroad regulation, formed the Greenback Party whose influence declined by the mid-1880s when most rejoined the Democratic and Republican parties.

The Farmers' Alliance

As the Grange and Greenbackers wilted, the Farmers' Alliance of Lampasas County began in 1877 and eventually spread nationwide, attracting between one and three million members. It supported labor and opposed land sharks and other capitalists. Lecturers and preachers spread its gospel throughout the South. "The farmers seem like unto ripe fruit," its board reported. "You can garner them by a gentle shake of the bush." The Farmers' Alliance became more active politically, especially at the 1886 convention where it adopted the Cleburne Demands, which included the regulation of interstate commerce among railroads and banking reforms.

These grass-roots groups spurred more changes, such as The Farmer's Alliance Exchange of Texas in Dallas, which carried everything from farm supplies to dry goods and groceries. Its members could sell cotton in lots at auction. This boosted state membership to over 150,000. Trouble brewed when cotton prices fell, and many farmers couldn't pay cash for goods or even a $2.00 assessment fee. Hard times also hit wool growers when wool dropped from eighteen to six and eight cents a pound. Because the Exchange lacked sufficient operating funds, it became a risky investment for banks which refused loans. Wholesalers, likewise, sided with stable merchants instead of the cooperative, and attempts by the Exchange to buy directly from manufacturers also failed because they wanted cash in return for cut-rate prices. And so the Alliance also began a rapid decline.

HOGG'S LAWS

James Stephen Hogg, the most colorful Texas politician since Sam Houston, stumped his way to the governor's office in 1891 by attacking capitalists and appealing to common people through homespun rhetoric. His style differed from recent predecessors. Governor John Ireland (1883-1887), an isolationist known as Oxcart John, had sought a return to the good old days when people lived in log cabins and used ox carts. Brigadier General Sullivan Ross (1887-1891) had fought wild Indians. Neither stood a chance against Hogg.

Chapter X: The New Gospel of Political Salvation

Governor James Stephen Hogg

The animated Hogg stood for radical reform. He opposed the national banking system, embraced the free coinage of silver, and sought honest railroad practices, a platform that spawned enemies, especially business interests. When he ran for governor the second time, he remarked: "There are lots of fellows opposing me. Some men oppose me because I was born in Texas, some oppose me because I am rather thick in the waist [he weighed around 250 pounds], some oppose me because I have eyes, and some oppose me on general principles." When stumping in the heat, he would take off his coat, loosen his suspenders, and drink water from a bucket—actions that endeared him to rural farmers.

As attorney general, Hogg had cleaned up dishonest insurance companies and saved the state over one million dollars. He even attacked Jay Gould's Texas Traffic Association, which pooled resources to set prices and control railroad operations. After the federal government passed the Interstate Commerce Act in 1887, Hogg got Texas to do likewise and made price fixing illegal. As one newspaper editor described him: "The Attorney General hangs his hat upon a peg, places his huge corporal avoirdupois in a big chair and works like a Trojan, and all violators of the law, whether they be railroad magnates or cattle kinds, know that he means business."

As governor, Hogg and his successor, Attorney General Charles A. Culberson, continued his fight against corrupt corporations. Hogg passed a land law that forced aliens—meaning Northern and European capitalists—to sell off their state holdings within six years, and another land law that made corporations dispose of unused real estate within fifteen years.

The 1891 Railroad Commission became his most notable feat. Hogg appointed John H. Reagan, a U.S. senator and co-author of the Interstate Commerce Act, as commissioner. "I want a man at the head of the commission that everybody knows to be clean and honest," he said. "And by gatlins, I would take the dust from the window sills of the skies to polish up the commission. It must be above reproach." The commissioners could fix freight rates and passenger fares. Although railroad robber barons filed an injunction that strapped progress for nearly two years, the Supreme Court finally gave Reagan the power to set rates. Some Texans wanted him to run for governor. He accepted but then withdrew as a candidate, remaining chairman of the Railroad Commission, which also became the state's regulatory agency for oil and gas.

After being reelected in 1892, Hogg continued to correct abuses. The railroads, for example, not only cut back on expansion but valued properties for a fraction of their worth in order to evade taxes. This provoked Hogg. His other reforms included making more land available to Texans, changing laws regarding pardons for prisoners, limiting city debts, lengthening the school year from four to six months, and supporting more funds for public schools and colleges. One faction called him "a gigantic swashbuckler of more tongue than brains," and a newspaper accused him of being the "completest [sic] and most perfect specimen of the demagogue that the nineteenth and all other centuries have produced." Hogg left office nearly broke but later made a fortune in oil.

THE PEOPLE'S PARTY

The Farmers' Alliance held grievances against Hogg. He hadn't appointed a farmer to the Railroad Commission and opposed both the subtreasury plan and government ownership of railroads. So they formed the People's Party (Populist Party) in 1891, which took chunks of its platform from the Granger movement, the Greenback Party, and the Alliance. It crusaded for railway and trust regulation. A political war followed in which the have-not Populists stumped at camp meetings and revivals, attacking Yankee capitalists as well as the affluent class in Texas—anyone who opposed reforms such as free coinage of silver and the sub-treasury plan which would allow them to store crops in government warehouses and get loans against market value. One newspaper wrote that Populists went "out into the hills and down into the valleys preaching their new gospel of political salvation."

The radical People's Party failed for several reasons—mostly because its popular platform lacked a sound core. In order to get votes, they

CHAPTER X: The New Gospel of Political Salvation

aligned themselves with black Texans, which alienated many party members and later caused a backlash against black rights. They also failed to gain support from Mexican Texans. Then the Democratic Party, which included most of its principles into its planks during the late 1890s, also fought prohibition and women's suffrage, two burning issues of the age. Ministers ranted against such evils from the pulpit. Yet anti-prohibitionists included former Governors Roberts, Throckmorton, and Coke, as well as former Confederate President Jefferson Davis. Voters defeated this amendment in 1887 as well as one for women's suffrage.

On the national level, Populists supported Democratic candidate William Jennings Bryan for president over Republican William McKinley because he endorsed free silver and low tariffs. Bryan is still famous for the statement: "You shall not press down upon the brow of labor this crown of thorns [the gold standard]; you shall not crucify mankind on a cross of gold." McKinley's election stripped the Populists of a leader and many rejoined the Republican Party or socialist movement. Renewed prosperity resulting from crop failures in Europe and the Klondike Gold Rush ended many grievances, and the third party crumbled, although the financial situation of small cotton farmers remained dire.

PUBLIC SERVICES

The railroads and agricultural products such as cotton and cottonseed oil helped Texas get back on its feet during the 1880s—but few banks lent money. One way the state financed schools and government buildings was through its public land policy. Railroads, of course, received enormous land grants, which accounted for their rapid growth. The Fifty-Cent Law of 1879 enabled speculators to buy land for $.50 an acre until its repeal. Politicians built the state capitol in Austin between 1883 and 1888 by selling three million acres on the High Plains to several Chicago brothers who started the famous XIT ranch which spread over two hundred miles. The Texas State Capitol Building, second in size only to the national Capitol in Washington, D.C. was considered the seventh largest building in the world when completed in 1888. Its construction involved one thousand laborers. Convicts cut and shaped the 15,700 carloads of red granite, some stones weighing up to twenty-five tons, brought on a railroad built for this purpose. The builders faced many hurdles, including a boycott, a rift with the architect, and the fear that the building might collapse. This grand edifice epitomizes the adage that everything is bigger in Texas.

Land grants also played a key role in the growth of Texas universities.

Texas state capitol in present-day downtown Austin

Politicians saw the need for higher education in the 1820s when they inserted in the Constitution of Coahuila and Texas an article for educational improvements. Later the Congress of the Republic reaffirmed this need and set aside around 17,000 acres in each county for public schools and 230,000 acres for two universities, but nothing happened until the legislature created the University of Texas. Secession and the Civil War held back its completion. It wasn't until 1876 that the Agricultural and Mechanical College of Texas (now Texas A&M University) started. The state's first institute for public school teachers, Sam Houston Normal Institute, also opened that year in Huntsville. The University of Texas began in 1883. Public schools, however, limped along because many counties failed to fund them.

Texans may have lagged behind many other states when the 20th century dawned, but a discovery at Beaumont made the lone star shine brightly overnight. And that was oil!

Chapter XI

Rigs of Prosperity

"Its equal cannot be seen on this earth."
—Anthony F. Lucas

Oil changed Texas forever. In the early 1890s, the entire state only produced around sixty barrels per years. Yet by 1904 investors had pumped $34,000,000 into wells! Fifty years later, this land contained the largest oil and gas fields in the world providing 55 percent of the country's reserves of crude oil. It had 37,000 miles of oil pipelines, 95 refineries, 199 natural gasoline plants, and 13,250 miles of gas pipeline.

Early explorers such as De Soto had caulked seams of boats with petroleum tar found near Sabine Pass. Later Indians and settlers of the Texas Gulf Coast used crude oil to preserve leather, as an ointment, and to lubricate the axles of wagons. They also used oil seeps from springs for medicinal purposes. In 1859 several ranchers dug wells but then stopped during the Civil War. Afterwards, more prospectors became interested in oil deposits, although none found a gusher. Most farmers sought a reliable water supply for cattle and agricultural products and considered oil a nuisance.

The first commercial production of oil started in 1895 when investors John H. Galey and James M. Guffey of Pennsylvania agreed to finance five test wells in Corsicana, a cotton town sixty miles south of Dallas. Although none became gushers, other drillers, gamblers, and speculators, including Joseph Stephen Cullinan, a former partner of John D. Rockefeller's Standard Oil, brought prosperity to the town. By 1899 wells produced over 600,000 barrels of oil a year, around one-ninetieth of the

Famous photo of Lucas gusher taken on January 10, 1901

country's output, but lacked storage tanks, refineries, and transportation facilities such as railroad cars. Galey and Guffey sold their interests. Some investors also questioned the fuel costs of oil and preferred cheaper coal or wood products.

Politicians such as former governor James Stephen Hogg worried about outside trusts and monopolies getting a foothold in the state. This resulted in a series of indictments against John D. Rockefeller and other moguls, which ended in Standard Oil paying several million dollars. (At the time they controlled 90 percent of oil refining in the country.) When Easterners reapplied for another charter, Hogg asked at the State Democratic Convention, "Shall Texas, or the trusts control?" Then he added: "We finally have a hold on the tail of the slimy serpent and they should not let it get hidden [again] in the tall grass."

Meanwhile, in Beaumont, a lumber town on the Neches River two hundred miles south of Corsicana, a jack-of-all-trades named Patillo Higgins believed petroleum existed under nearby salt dome formations. He purchased tracts around the Big Hill area south of town and in 1892 convinced several investors to back the Gladys City Oil, Gas, and Manufacturing Company, hoping to turn it into an inland manufacturing center. When funds ran out, the project bottomed up, helped along by the 1893 depression. Higgins then tried to interest Standard Oil, but they ridiculed the idea. Undaunted, he advertised and received a positive response from Anthony Lucas, a native of Austria with a degree in engineering. After drilling nearly six hundred feet without success, he sought outside capital from wildcatters Galey and Guffey, who got financial wizard Andrew Mellon's backing. The desperate Lucas agreed to keep the agreement secret, lease land around the salt dome, and remove Higgins as a partner, which ended their relationship. Higgins later sued and received a settlement.

The rest seems lifted from some dime novel. Although contractors had trouble with quicksand and gas pressure, they finally hit oil at around twelve hundred feet on January 10, 1901. A well suddenly blew out six tons of pipe, which carried away part of the upper derrick (framework over an oil well) and then crashed to the ground. For nine days the Lucas Gusher spewed around 800,000 barrels of crude oil a day until they managed to cap it. Overnight oil fever hit Beaumont, a leading lumber center and railroad crossroads, which one newspaper called "the Houston of East Texas." Its population mushroomed from nine thousand to fifty thousand as prospectors, conmen, and roughnecks invaded the town looking for fast profits. Grocery stores stayed open around the clock. Speculators filled every hotel and rooming house, sleeping in barber chairs, on billiard ta-

Panorama of oil derricks at Spindletop

bles, and even in bathtubs. The town's packed hotel, the Crosby House, looked like a stock exchange. "Oil insanity [was] strictly monomania," said a member of the Beaumont Oil Exchange and Board of Trade, adding that "they heard nothing but oil and they talked nothing but oil."

Spindletop (a popular name for the hill where they discovered oil) at Beaumont and other oil towns were eyesores. Shacks stood on stilts. Flies and mosquitoes spread malaria, filth caused typhoid and dysentery, and oil and gas fumes bred lung problems. Oil and mud soaked everything—streets, houses, people. As one doctor wrote: "Mud and water was sloshing in my sock as I walked … I glanced up from my mud-laden legs and there, in that mire which was called a street, were men, up to their knees in the mud and water, driving mule and ox-teams carrying heavy machinery which sank the wheels down to their hubs. Some of the men were laughing, others singing, and some were swearing."

Trains of sightseers came to gawk at the well sites and spouting oil. Hustlers hawked wares on street corners. Saloons, gambling dens, and dance halls spouted faster than oil rigs. So did the "red light" district. It was another California or Klondike gold rush. Things got so bad the chief of police finally told people to carry a gun.

Chapter XI: Rigs of Prosperity

The hill soon became known as "Swindletop." Fortunes were made and lost in hours. Pig wallows went for $35,000 and cow pastures for $100,000 to oil syndicates. A printer who bought and sold a lease in one day made $30,000. Owners laughed at one speculator who offered $1,000,000 for an acre of land worth less than $100 a year earlier. Some tracts were divided into 25 by 25 feet. Captain Lucas said that four companies capitalized at $1,000,000 only held rights to a tract 45 by 45 feet. By 1901 over four hundred wells covered the hill at Spindletop. Wealthy investors such as the Hogg-Swayne Syndicate, as well as eastern capital, soon controlled most properties. The state chartered five hundred companies. Prices, however, fluctuated wildly because of over production and lack of marketing outlets. Texas needed pipelines and refineries, which cost a fortune and forced developers to seek funds from northern investors.

Oil production soon declined at Spindletop because of over drilling, although in 1927 a second oil craze produced 21,250,000 barrels. Spindletop's early fertile fields not only launched Gulf Coast exploration, but reduced the influence of Standard Oil's monopoly and started the age of liquid fuel. In 1904, the fourteen hundred locomotives of Southern Pacific Railroad converted from coal to oil burners. The rise of automobile production from four thousand in 1900 to over two million in 1920 also increased the need for oil.

After Spindletop, the early oil craze moved to other boomtowns such as Sour Lake, Batson, Saratoga, and Humble. Wildcatters drilled wherever they found oil spills or salt domes and invested fortunes, digging over three thousand wells with derricks so close that some touched. Texas Gulf Coast fields had pumped around ninety million barrels of oil, and future giants of the petroleum industry such as Gulf Oil, Mobil, and Texaco had launched their mega-empires. Another oil bonanza followed in the west Texas Panhandle fields during the 1920s when four-fifths of its counties discovered oil and gas deposits, turning the area from a frontier into a cluster of industrially oriented centers. The same happened in east Texas in the 1930s, where wildcat wells produced over one million barrels a day. The natural gas industry also exploded in Texas—all of which led to enormous economic growth before World War II.

THE RISE OF CITIES

The population of Texas increased five-fold between the Civil War and 1900—from 600,000 to around 3 million. One-fourth of the population came from other states and 200,000 from abroad. Although still primarily agricultural, nearly 20 percent of its people now lived in urban areas because of industrialization. The five largest cities in 1900 were San Antonio, Dallas, Fort Worth, Galveston, and Houston.

San Antonio

Still the state's largest city in 1900 with 53,000 people, San Antonio remained a center of diverse ethnic richness. In 1854, Frederick Law Olmstead wrote that no other city except New Orleans had such a "jumble of races, costumes, languages and buildings." By the century's turn, it celebrated everything from German fall Volkfests to Carnival Week with its parades and festivals to the annual San Antonio International Fair. Leather factories, flour mills, and breweries provided work for its growing population, which reached 230,000 by 1930. The city also became a military center. Here, Teddy Roosevelt trained the Rough Riders during the Spanish-American War. Fort Sam Houston, the region's largest post, housed generals such as John J. Pershing before World War I, Arthur MacArthur (father of Douglas MacArthur), and Dwight D. Eisenhower.

Market Plaza in San Antonio with chili stand in the foreground

CHAPTER XI: Rigs of Prosperity

Dallas

Once the railroad connected this city with Houston in 1872, Dallas became a center for the cotton, farm machinery, and buffalo-hide markets. It was known as the world's largest inland cotton market. Expanding industry, food-processing plants, and oil soon made it the financial center of the Southwest as well as a cultural center. In 1914, the city housed the 11th District Federal Reserve Bank. The Ford Motor Company opened a plant there, and construction of the five million dollar Union Passenger Terminal train station began, which eventually served a dozen railroads.

Fort Worth

The "Queen City of the Prairie" became a stopover for cattle drives heading for Kansas City and soon developed into the packing-house center of the Southwest when Armour and Swift opened plants. Cowboys in dusters and high-heeled boots bought supplies there and spent money freely in stores and saloons. After the discovery of oil, the city also became a center for petroleum companies and later for the aviation business.

Galveston

In the 1870s when Comanches were still raiding towns in the Panhandle, Galveston had become a prosperous city that rivaled many in the Northeast. The city started a telephone exchange in 1881, in 1882 it strung electric lights, and in 1891 it used electricity for streetcars. At the century's turn, Galveston had become the country's third busiest port as well as an important grain exporter, besides a rival of nearby Houston for economic control of the region. During 1899 and 1900, its port generated a staggering $220 million in business, making it one of the country's richest places. One newspaper called this city of 38,000 "the New York of the Gulf." It showcased beaches, elegant hotels, and fabulous mansions such as the four-story Gresham house. In addition, newspapers, theaters, and sporting events such as horse racing also made Galveston a cultural center, especially for members of the elitist class who controlled the island.

All this changed after September 9, 1900. The historic Galveston hurricane ravaged the city and claimed around six thousand lives, besides many more on the mainland. The Texas coast had been hit by other storms. Several in 1875 and 1886 wrecked Indianola, located on Matagorda Bay. Three hit Galveston in 1871. Prominent leaders recognized the city's vulnerability and talked about building a seawall, but nothing had ever happened. Some scientists even believed the city could withstand any storm because of its sandbars, shallow water, and houses on stilts. Confident that they could weather this storm as they had others, Galvestonians ignored warnings and went about their business, some children even playing near the water. By early afternoon, however, people had grown concerned when the bay waters continued to rise and winds tore up bathhouses. Waves soon reached the tops of telephone poles. Evacuation from the island ended when water covered the wagon bridge and three railroad bridges, submerging Galveston and cutting it off from the state. Telegraph wires went dead. Debris crushed and twisted houses as wind gusts reached 120 miles per hour and waves rose to 25 feet. People ran for high ground and sought safety in churches, upper stories, and municipal buildings. The 220-foot tower of St. Patrick's Church crashed. The roof of St. Mary's Orphanage caved in, killing nearly a hundred children. Many palatial mansions were turned into rubble. One person recalled that "we could hear houses crashing under the impact of the wreckage hurled forward by the wind and storm tide, but this did not blot out the screams of the injured and dying."

The hurricane's aftermath was horrendous. Galveston lay in ruins—thirty-six hundred homes destroyed along with hundreds of other buildings—while railroad tracks, the docks, and streets seemed beyond repair. Thousands lost their homes and possessions. Many lacked food, clothes, or medicine. The mayor declared martial law and ordered militiamen to shoot looters. Dead bodies were heaped everywhere. Decomposed remains of those taken on barges into the Gulf of Mexico washed ashore and were buried in sand, while hundreds of others found in the wreckage were cremated. A teenager later recalled: "There were so many dead, you would sink into the silt onto a body at every other step." Emergency relief arrived from everywhere, over a million dollars' worth. The elderly Clara Barton, president of the American National Red Cross, came to Galveston with nurses and workers. A relief committee set up stations that rationed food and supplies, tried to find shelter for the homeless, and appointed cleanup squads. The task seemed overwhelming. A former state senator reported: "Great piles of human bodies, dead animals, rotting vegetation, household furniture and fragments of the houses themselves are piled in confused heaps right in the main streets of the city." The hurricane caused around thirty million dollars in damage and became the country's worst disaster in its history. Although property values decreased and thousands left, the city built a three-mile seawall of concrete and eventually recovered economically. But Houston had now become the state's most important city.

Chapter XI: Rigs of Prosperity

Photo of downtown Houston around 1900

Houston

Houston's population had doubled every ten years after the Civil War. People called it the place "Where Eleven Railroads Meet the Sea." Lumber, rice, and cotton brought great wealth to the city, with a combined capital of 1,455 million dollars in 1912, not including railroads, banks, and trust companies. Oil helped total bank clearances reach one billion dollars in 1906. The later water channel, which linked Houston with Galveston Bay, offered direct access to the Gulf of Mexico, making it a world-class port. All this resulted in a flurry of new building during the early 20th century, which ranged from the Carnegie Library to neo-classical and gingerbread Victorian mansions with turrets, stained-glass windows, and iron lions on the front lawns. The city's population eventually exceeded that of San Antonio.

ETHNIC SALAD BOWL

Texas has always been a salad bowl of different ethnic and cultural groups. As one historian has pointed out, "The Texian victors of 1836 lived in Finnish log cabins, fought with German long rifles, drank Scottish whiskey, adhered to British dissenter Protestantism, and introduced the language of common law of England. Walk among their tombstones in the graveyards of rural Texas and you will find the Scotch-Irish McLane and Ross, the Germans Snider and Buckner, the English Alsbury and Cooper, the Dutch De Witt and Kuykendall, the Welsh Williams and Jones, the Huguenots Lamar and Alley, the Swedes Swanson and Justice."

BLACK TEXANS

Most black Texans worked as sharecroppers or tenant farmers, earning a meager income and finding it hard to get loans or purchase land. Those who moved to cities worked as domestic servants, laborers, and on the railroad. Longshoremen and lumbermen did better because of labor unions. Fewer than 5 percent were craftsmen or professionals, mostly ministers or teachers.

Limited educational opportunities handicapped black Texans. The state founded Prairie View Agricultural and Mechanical College (1878), connected to Texas A&M, which offered degrees in educational and vocational training for blacks. It wasn't until Houston College opened in 1947 that another black state university existed. Some teachers attended college courses to fulfill certification requirements. Few secondary schools provided for black Texans, so students rarely went beyond sixth or eighth grade. Even though they were supposed to get separate but equal attention, this seldom happened for several reasons. Many districts refused to levy local school taxes to educate blacks or, for that matter, even provide adequate facilities for Anglo Texans. Black Texan schools also received fewer funds which resulted in run-down quarters, inadequate supplies, and unqualified teachers.

Race relations between white and black Texans worsened at the century's turn. The Populists used racial issues to get black Texan support and then ignored them. Laws undermined black social and political influence, helped along by the U.S. Supreme Court's ruling in the 1896 *Plessy vs Ferguson* case that legalized separate public facilities. Segregation became a way of life: separate sections on trains, streets, and in theaters, separate drinking fountains and restrooms, separate waiting rooms, separate places in town to live. Cohabitation among the races also became unlawful. As late as 1933, Houston authorities turned down plans for the new Southern Pacific railroad station because black and Anglo Texans would use the same ramps. Discrimination spread.

In 1910 politicians wanted to repeal the Fifteenth Amendment to prevent black Texans from voting. In response to such discrimination, blacks created their own community cultures. They celebrated Juneteenth and opened saloons, parks, and theaters. They attended their own religious services. (Nearly 400,000 black Texans belonged to a church in 1916.) They also formed organizations such as the Negro Business League, the Knights of Pythias, and a chapter of the NAACP.

The law also turned its back on black Texans. Those who couldn't post bonds waited in jail for weeks or months and received longer sentences. Some served time to pay fines. Violence soon flared. Anglo Texans burned a black section of town in Longview and two amusement parks in Beaumont. Lynchings continued—nearly four hundred between 1882 and 1927. Governor Hogg unsuccessfully sought an anti-lynching law in 1892 after a mob burned and mutilated a black Texan male. In another instance, a black accused of murder and rape was found guilty and given a death sentence. Vigilantes rushed the courtroom and took the condemned to a tree where they maimed and burned him alive, then dragged his remains through town. The rise of the Ku Klux Klan in the 1920s aggravated matters.

A few black Texans managed to make a mark on society, especially as musicians and athletes. Cowboy Charles Willis wrote the famous ballad, "Goodbye Old Paint" which helped immortalize western folklore. Blind Lemon Jefferson became known as King of the Country Blues, and Huddie Leadbelly Jefferson composed "C.C. Rider," "Midnight Special," and "Goodnight Irene." Famed ragtime musician Scott Joplin from Texarkana wrote the "Maple Leaf Rag," and Euday L. Bowman wrote "Twelfth Street Rag." Boxer Jack Johnson became the world's heavyweight champion in 1910, and baseball pitcher Andrew Rube Foster organized the Negro National League in 1920. One black entrepreneur, Hobart Taylor, even became a millionaire by investing in taxicabs and an insurance company.

MEXICAN TEXANS

The lives of Mexican Texans generally mirrored the black experience—being treated as second-class citizens. In 1910 around 233,000 people of Mexican descent lived in Texas, many still in the same area as 1887—south counties near the Rio Grande. Several factors, however, led to their increase: the Mexican Revolution of 1909-10, the International and Great Northern Railroad that linked Laredo with San Antonio, and the switch from ranching to farming near the San Antonio River. All three set the stage for more Mexicans to cross the border and begin a new life in the U.S. Most, of course, remained in the southern part of the state to be nearer their families. That's also where they found the most work as domestics and farm laborers.

Most Mexican Texan laborers picked cotton, vegetables, and fruit during the "immigration generation," alongside black and Anglo Texan renters. Others became sheepshearers and lumberjacks, or labored in the oil fields. Thousands also worked in textile mills, construction, and cotton compresses after the Houston Ship Channel opened. Between 1900 and 1920, Mexican Texans made up around three-fourths of all railroad workers. Most earned low wages. Language and cultural differences limited their assimilation into the Anglo Texan culture that dominated politics and economics. Many women stayed on farms or did domestic work instead of attending school. Most Mexicans who moved to cities lived in downtrodden sections, which isolated their children and limited change. Businesses put up signs that read: "No Mexicans or Dogs allowed."

The rapid growth of investment companies and mechanized farming between 1910 and 1930 caused clashes between old settlers and newcomers. The political power of landowners slipped away because of increased taxes, the failing cattle and sheep market, and swindlers. Even landed Mexican Texan ranchers were treated as inferiors and without respect as farming replaced stock raising. David Montejano points out in *Anglos and Mexicans in the Making of Texas 1836-1986*: "The newly arrived Americans did not distinguish between the aristocratic and laboring classes—to Americans both types are the same—Mexicans … Even among former *vaqueros* and *peones*, the displaced elite, which had prided itself as being Castilian, was now commonly referred to as '*los tuvos*'—'the has-beens.' In the rural society these commercial farmers were creating, there were no longer any significant differences between the displaced 'Spanish' elite and the landless 'Mexican.' Now a Mexican was simply a Mexican."

The Mexican Revolution of 1910 crystallized conflicts that had been festering for nearly one hundred years. Mexicans had rebelled against Spanish oppression in 1819 and then against the feudal colonial system during the American Civil War period in which leader Benito Juarez rose to power. The bloody 1910 revolution sought to oust dictator Don Porfirio Diaz and do away with the plantation system controlled by rich privileged persons who enslaved the poor. As a result, thousands migrated to Texas to escape Mexico's corrupt government and technologically weak agricultural economy.

The "boss system" of powerful ranchers also stripped Mexican Texans of political power by pressuring registered workers to vote for chosen candidates, a strategy some elitist Mexican Texan families supported. These politicians passed laws and a poll tax which required cash to vote. City elections also helped reduce *barrio* representation in government. Mexican Texans responded to such injustices by joining organizations, forming unions, and enrolling in *mutualistas* or aid societies which helped cement group identity. Others signed the Plan de San Diego in support of a race war against Anglo Texans in order to create another independent republic in the Spanish Southwest. More violence erupted. This plan failed when the state called in Texas Rangers.

The World War I boom and the Immigration Act of 1917 (which severely cut immigration quotas from Europe) caused a critical need for migrant workers. As one newspaper editor asked, "Where is the country going to get labor?" He answered that "the doors are already open to Mexicans." Several hundred thousand fled to Texas who were caught in a bind: distrusting the Mexican government that preached democracy but failed to practice it, or being exploited by landowners and large-scale farmers. Few became naturalized citizens compared to other foreign-born immigrants—5.5 percent as opposed to 49.7—for several reasons: discrimination, illegal entry into the U.S., and the plan to return home after saving enough money. It also took the average immigrant fifteen years to become a citizen.

European Texans

Many European ethnic groups also came to Texas during the 19th century—nearly 350,000 by 1910—and were greater strangers to the borderland than black and Mexican Texans with their curious clothes, languages, foods, and old-world customs. German Texans, for instance, made up one-third of San Antonio's population by 1880 and comprised the state's largest ethnic group next to blacks. Czechs, Silesians, and Wends (Sorbs) settled in the south-central part of Texas. Poles founded the country's first Polish settlement in Panna Maria in 1854.

These settlers left their homelands because of wars, famine, discrimination, tax burdens, and for adventure. Land was cheap in Texas. The "first wave" came between 1831 and 1869, mostly Irish and Germans. Immigration slowed during the Civil War. Then a spurt followed which became known as the great immigration. The Texas Alien Land Law of 1892, however, wronged many groups because it prevented immigrants from buying land and forced them to become U.S. citizens within ten years. Prejudice led some of these people to return home. Others stayed, struggled, and eventually became part of the Texas legacy. With the rise of mechanized agriculture, many of these people also moved from rural areas to cities and got jobs as laborers, worked in the oil fields, or started small stores.

Chapter XII

Where the Chicken Got the Axe

"People in Texas are going hog wild over education. I don't mind higher education, just so long as it doesn't go too high."
—Governor James E. Ferguson

The population of Texas doubled between 1890 and 1920. Yet in essence, it remained a Southern agricultural state—a reality soon changed by the discovery of oil, immigration, and city growth. By 1920 San Antonio, Houston, Dallas, and Fort Worth all boasted populations greater than 100,000. Houston became the leading cotton port in the country, and eastern investors now wanted to sink their teeth into the lumber industry and petroleum. The spread of railroads and rise of the automobile also helped alter the state's rural-to-urban landscape.

PROGRESSIVE POLITICS

A progressive reform movement began to dislodge the Populists of the late 19th century. Politicians preached about industrial corruption, the plight of rural workers, prohibition, and even women's right to vote. Yet in some ways, Texas differed from other parts of the country—maintaining an anti-Eastern attitude, and considering immigrants, the uneducated, and minorities a threat to their goals. So while progressive in some ways, this period still remained biased and conservative. As one local said in the 1920s about Mexican Texans, "If a Mexican bought a lot among the whites, they would burn him out. We are just old, hard-boiled southerners in this county."

Wealthy Texan E. M. House became interested in diplomacy during this time and worked as a political consultant for two decades. After supporting Governor Hogg—who dubbed him "Colonel" in 1892—House formed a faction of power brokers called "our crowd" who pulled political strings. He managed the gubernatorial campaigns of Charles A. Culberson (1895-1899), Joseph D. Sayers (1899-1903), and S. W. T. Lanham (1903-1907). He then moved to New York and met Woodrow Wilson, becoming his "dearest friend" and personal advisor. *Harper's Weekly* called him "Assistant President House" and *Collier's* described him as the president's "Silent Partner." Wilson's crimped campaign needed a Texas victory to assure the election. During World War I, House helped draft the Fourteen Points, a constitution for the League of Nations, and served as Wilson's chief deputy at the Paris Peace Conference in 1919. But he wanted more public power, making cutting diary comments such as "The President lacks executive ability and does not get the best results from his Cabinet or those around him. Therefore they come to me and I have to do it at long-range which is difficult and unsatisfactory." Grasping the political overtones, Wilson cut ties with House after the peace treaty.

With the help of House, former Confederate conservatives Sayers and Lanham became Texas governors during a period of expanding business interests. As governor, Sayers handled the Huntsville Penitentiary fire of 1899, the Brazos River flood of 1899, and the historical Galveston storm of 1900. The Lanham administration pushed through reforms that included the chartering of banks, raising taxes of railroad assets, and enforcing antitrust suits. The legislature under Lanham also passed the Terrell Election Law in 1905, which states nominees for office would be chosen through primaries rather than by convention, and all parties that polled at least 100,000 votes in the last election would hold primaries the fourth Saturday in July. A poll tax was also required to vote in primaries—which excluded many poor Anglo Texans as well as Mexican and black Texans. All-white primaries weren't outlawed until 1944, and the poll tax remained until 1966.

Politics wasn't the only area of stormy change in early-20th-century Texas. The most important antitrust suit during this period involved the Waters-Pierce Case. The U.S. Supreme Court upheld a Texas suit that convicted this company of being tied to Standard Oil and revoked its Texas license. Senator Joseph W. Bailey managed to get them a new permit. When the state of Missouri brought suit against Waters-Pierce in 1906 for being connected to the Standard Oil trust, Texas filed another suit, which resulted in the company's license being revoked again, fines of over $1,800,000, and the sale of the company's state property. Senator

Bailey, investigated for his relationship with Waters-Pierce, withdrew from the next Senate race in 1912.

Governor Thomas M. Campbell (1907-1911), a disciple of Theodore Roosevelt, spouted that trusts and taxes were "bleeding the people" and that he wanted to stop such enemies from "dragging their slimy trail over" the state. He also called lobbyists "the hired instruments of selfish schemes." The Robertson Insurance Law (1907) forced life insurance companies to invest 75 percent of their reserves in Texas securities and real estate. Campbell's administration not only enacted prison laws and municipal government changes, but created state agencies such as the departments of banking, health, licensing and regulation. The Texas State Library also began during this period.

The anti-prohibition stand of Campbell's successor, Governor Oscar Branch Colquitt (1911-1915), distanced him from many progressives and led temperance groups to call him the champion of "Demon Rum." He continued with penal reforms and pushed through the first state workmen's compensation law. Most hurdles of his administration involved state deficits and Rio Grande border clashes stemming from the Mexican Revolution of 1910.

Me and Ma

In 1914, self-made banker Jim Ferguson suddenly and unexpectedly campaigned for governor, appealing to the plight of workers and tenant farmers. His simple plank announced: "Whereas, I, James E. Ferguson, am as well qualified to be Governor of Texas as any damn man in it; and Whereas, I am against prohibition and always will be; and Whereas, I am in favor of a square deal for tenant farmers: Therefore Be It Resolved that I will be elected." He won against formidable odds through a cracker-barrel style of rhetoric with grassroots appeal. "Pa" or "Farmer Jim" made it known he would veto any bill that involved prohibition "where the chicken got the axe," called tenant farmers "the boys at the forks of the creek," and said his opponent "voted dry, but drank wet." As one supporter put it, "He spoke the language of the corn rows and the vernacular of the country stores."

During his first term, Ferguson attacked the Ku Klux Klan, got a state department of forestry started, and pushed a farm tenancy bill that regulated tenant farmer rent to one-fourth the value of cotton and one-third the value of grain produced, although the courts later struck down this law. He also supported compulsory school attendance, highways, and child labor reforms. After being reelected, Ferguson created more educa-

Governors James E. Ferguson and Miriam A. Ferguson, ca.1928

tional reforms and a state highway commission, which limited speeding to fifteen miles an hour in cities and eighteen miles an hour in rural areas. Then he tangled with the University of Texas when the board of regents refused to remove certain members of the faculty, fire the president, and let Ferguson control parts of the budget. As a result, he vetoed program funds. This set off a hornet's nest of protest from alumni of the university who called for impeachment and got support from backers of prohibition and women's suffrage. It resulted in the governor's indictment on ten out of twenty-one charges. The Senate, which Ferguson called a kangaroo court, removed him from office for misapplication of funds and barred him from holding any state office—a decree the governor ignored. He later unsuccessfully ran for governor again, calling the University of Texas faculty "educated fools," "butterfly chasers," and "two-bit thieves" controlled by administrators. He also failed to win the U.S. presidency on the American Party ticket (1920) and a senate seat (1922).

Ferguson refused to quit politics and in 1924 and 1932 ran campaigns to put his wife, Miriam, in the governor's seat as his mouthpiece. Ferguson promised that "in short, the people of Texas will have two governors for the price of one!" Campaign posters and car stickers read "Me and Ma." Miriam not only became the first woman governor of Texas but the first elected woman governor in the U.S. "Pa" Ferguson's desk was right next to hers where he made most political decisions. Although "Ma" Ferguson failed to reduce state expenditures and gave too many pardons, she attacked the Ku Klux Klan at a time when many office holders in the state supported its spread.

PROGRESSIVE EXPANSIONISM

During the progressive period at century's turn, the U.S. became a power player in world affairs through three conflicts: The Spanish-American War, border clashes with Mexico, and World War I. The defeat of old-world power Spain not only increased U.S. confidence but gained respect from Britain, France, Germany, and Russia. Border friction with Mexico on the Rio Grande during the revolution provided more printers' ink for the newspaper chains of Joseph Pulitzer and William Randolph Hearst. For example, it's said that during the Spanish-American War, Hearst telegrammed illustrator Frederick Remington: "You furnish the pictures, and I'll furnish the war." World War I saw the U.S. emerge as a formidable economic and political leader in international affairs, a role continued to the present age.

THE SPANISH-AMERICAN WAR

When Cuba revolted against Spain in the 1890s, the U.S. decided to intervene for several reasons. Spain mistreated Cuban citizens badly, subjecting the country to martial law and confining people to fenced demilitarized zones. U.S. businesses also had fifty million dollars invested in the country—mostly in sugar, iron, and tobacco—and wanted to promote trade. Then the USS *Maine*, in Cuba on a goodwill visit, sunk in Havana Harbor on February 16, 1898. Public outcries arose, leading the U.S. to declare war on Spain, even though a submarine mine probably caused the disaster.

Texas became a major army base for the Spanish-American War. Ten thousand men from Texas alone signed up for duty. The famous Rough Riders trained in San Antonio under Colonel Leonard Wood and Lieutenant Theodore Roosevelt. Dressed in slouch hats and blue bandannas, they made a strange lot, like their ancestors during the Republic's revolution. Roosevelt praised Texan soldiers as being good riders, trailers, and shots because of their life in the open. He later wrote about the Rough

Colonel Theodore Roosevelt training Rough Riders at the old Fair Grounds in San Antonio in 1898

Rider's rush up San Juan Hill: "I think we suffered more heavily than the Spaniards did in killed and wounded (though we also captured some scores of prisoners). It would have been very extraordinary if the reverse was the case, for we did the charging; and to carry earthworks on foot with dismounted cavalry, when these earthworks are held by unbroken infantry armed with best modern rifles, is a serious task."

BORDER CLASHES ON THE RIO GRANDE

Cattle thieves, bandits, and Mexicans found it easy to cross the Rio Grande and hide in the vast lower valley. Rebels not only found a market for smuggling and gunrunning, but also raided farms and ranches, hit railroad trains, and stole whatever they could find. Crooked Anglo Texan officials and law officers also smuggled goods and rustled cattle. Lawlessness became so bad that in 1911 President Taft mobilized an entire division of army troops at San Antonio to defend the border.

Things worsened after the tyrannical president of Mexico Porfirio Diaz resigned and went into exile. Revolutionary groups rose and fell in Mexico as violence spilled over into Texas. Clashes broke out between Mexican Texans and Anglo Texans. When this resulted in the Plan de San Diego— a radical attempt to ignite a rebellion on the part of Texas Mexicans—the U.S. strengthened forces on the Rio Grande while President Woodrow

Wilson followed a "watch and wait" policy. By 1916 most of the regular army and the National Guard were stationed at the border. Two factors confused issues: Wilson didn't recognize any Mexican regime, and although troops could enter Mexico in pursuit of raiders who crossed the Rio Grande, they couldn't invade another country. Texas Governor Colquitt, however, took action and sent in the Texas Rangers who incited more trouble.

Although President Wilson finally recognized the Mexican government, collisions continued. The raids of Pancho Villa along with the Plan de San Diego caused a risky "punitive expedition" by General John J. Pershing into Mexico to halt the bandit raids. Instead of prisoners, Pershing returned with refugees, including over four hundred Chinese. Then the Zimmerman Note (Telegram) sent by the German foreign minister to his ambassador in Mexico caused a sensation. It stated that if Mexico and Japan joined Germany and other Central Powers against the Allies, they would receive funds and lands at the end of World War I. The note, published internationally, helped inflame U.S. support for declaring war, which happened on April 6, 1917.

U.S. army punitive expedition into Mexico after Pancho Villa, 1916

The USS Texas *was the most powerful battleship in the world during World War I.*

World War I

In 1912 Democrat Woodrow Wilson became president and rewarded influential Texas political supporters with important posts. Albert Sidney Burleson became postmaster general, Thomas Watt Gregory U.S. attorney, Thomas B. Love assistant treasury secretary, David Houston secretary of agriculture, and E. M. House personal advisor. Sam Rayburn also began his career in the House of Representatives and Morris Sheppard, who introduced the Eighteenth Amendment (prohibition), started his rise to power in the Senate. When World War I erupted, these men stood behind Wilson.

Most Texans supported the war effort. One soldier fighting in France boasted: "Hell, this kind o' fightin's just a relaxation to me. I'm from San Angelo." Nearly 200,000 males from Texas saw service, 25 percent of them black. This didn't halt racism. Black Texans had recently been lynched in Huntsville, Temple, Waco, and Galveston. The Houston Riot of 1917 erupted when black Texan soldiers rioted against racial slurs and segregated buses while politicians and police turned their backs. These troops killed people and sent crowds into the "wild stage of paroxysms." Several hundred national guardsmen sealed off the riot section to prevent more bloodshed by vigilante groups. The largest court martial in U.S. history followed. Military tribunals hanged some mutinous soldiers and gave others life sentences in federal prison.

Give Till It Hurts

Texas played a key role in early aviation history. Pilot training began in 1910 when the Signal Corps sent its first plane and technicians under Benjamin D. Foulois to San Antonio with a $150 budget. "Old No. 1 came by express to San Antonio in seventeen wooden crates," Major General Foulois later wrote. "We worked on our craft in a shed on the cavalry parade ground to the gibers of hard-bitten cavalrymen. We were referred to as its 'crazed birdmen.'"

During World War I, the government established Kelly Field in San Antonio, which trained over 1,500 pilots and more than 32,000 officers and enlisted men, including Charles A. Lindbergh. In 1928 they built Randolph Field, the West Point of the Air, and until 1938 all Army Air Corps pilots trained at Texas air bases. San Antonio remained the hub of U.S. aviation until after World War II. In addition, the USS *Texas*, the most powerful ship in the world, also launched the first plane from an American battleship.

Many civilians pitched in to help the war effort. They didn't eat wheat on Mondays and Wednesdays, pork on Thursdays and Saturdays, or any meat at all on Tuesdays. People bought Liberty Bonds, Victory Bonds, and War Savings Stamps ("Do Your Bit" and "Give Till It Hurts"), as well as planted war gardens and joined organizations such as the Red Cross. Some women worked in factories. Almost five hundred nurses served in the war. Patriotism flourished. The state required all schools to fly the American flag, classes be taught in English, and at least ten minutes each day be spent on teaching patriotism. They removed books that praised German accomplishments from the shelves of schools, renamed sauerkraut "liberty cabbage," and Governor Hobby vetoed funds for the University of Texas German language department. Even the homes of Texas Germans were searched to find photos of the Kaiser. This contempt for Germans in Texas traced back to the antebellum era when they refused to own slaves and later sympathized with the Union during the Civil War.

Over five thousand Texans lost their lives during the Great War, nearly half because of the 1918 Spanish influenza epidemic. As a result, the government passed acts to help servicemen: property couldn't be sold until one year after discharge, returning soldiers were exempted from penalties on late taxes and the poll tax. They could also attend state colleges tuition free. Mexican Texans also served in the armed forces, helped on the home front, and became a part of local campaigns.

WOMEN'S SUFFRAGE MOVEMENT

The war also provided a lively platform for women's suffrage—although the going got tough. Most men and some women opposed such rights. Joe Bailey declared: "It would be useless to talk to a woman about the great and fundamental principles of government. To her way of thinking, no man should be permitted to do anything which she thinks a good man ought not to do." Yet women crusaders persisted. The Texas Woman Suffrage Association (1903) changed its name to the Texas Equal Suffrage Association and grew to nearly a hundred local societies by 1918. They were inspired by Mary Eleanor Brackenridge and Annette Finnegan once the Texas legislature permitted women to vote in primary elections. Reformers such as Minnie Fisher Cunningham (a founder of the National League of Women Voters and candidate for the U.S. senate in 1918 and governor in 1944) and Annie Webb Blanton (state superintendent of public instruction), among others, kept the pressure on politicians. In 1919 Texas became the first Southern state and the ninth in the nation to approve the Nineteenth Amendment (women's suffrage).

In addition to voting rights, the "petticoat lobby" also promoted educational and political reform. Women promoted the opening of the Texas State College for Women in 1903 and getting the legislature to require compulsory school attendance in 1915. Olga Kholberg started the first public kindergarten in El Paso in 1893. Jovita Idar did the same for San Antonio in 1917 and organized support for Mexican Texans. Anna Hertzberg founded San Antonio's first night school. And in 1918, Annie Webb Blanton became the state's first female superintendent of public instruction. Women also fought for prison reform, the juvenile court system, and prohibition.

RUM ON THE RUN

Even before the Civil War, Texans banned saloons, although repealing the law in 1856. Organizations such as The United Friends of Temperance, Women's Christian Temperance Union, and the Anti-Saloon League followed. Even a Prohibition Party rose in the 1880s. The "drys" made more headway in north and west Texas counties than in south and southeast ones. To halt the "dry" movement, the Retail Liquor Dealers' Association collected over two million dollars from members, but zealots continued the crusade. Even temperance activist Carrie Nation visited Texas, smashing up saloons with bricks and attacking those in a Galveston bar. "There you go pouring out some of that slop," she cried. "Men, you ought not to drink that stuff, it will ruin your liver and damn your souls."

The social gospel of Protestant fundamentalism tied most evils to alcohol. The Southern Baptist Convention, for example, predicted that with the end of liquor "to a large extent you abolish the gambling den and the den of vice, for these are found almost invariably in connection with the saloon. You abolish also many of the evils of the sweat shop, if not the sweat shop itself. You abolish child labor, for then the father will be able to earn a living for the family without forcing his children to labor to support themselves and him. You go far toward abolishing the crowded tenement, for with the father as the wage-earner each family will be able to have its own little home." One Baptist newspaper called the saloon keeper "an anarchist in the Kingdom of God" and said if they defeated the prohibition amendment, "every evil will be glad and reinvigorated, the powers of darkness will break forth on every side to overrun the county." When prohibition eventually became law, one evangelist performed a burial service over a pine casket filled with whiskey bottles.

The prohibition movement became so fierce that the Democratic Party

Women demonstrating in Lufkin for the passage of prohibition

broke into two groups: the "drys" and the "wets," one attacking the many abuses of alcohol, the other extolling the rights of free choice. Yet people voted against an amendment. Liquor, however, remained on the front burner of reform. The Texas Railroad Commission, the Robertson Insurance Law, and lumber abuses had all been addressed. Several scandals helped to renew efforts to "put rum on the run in Texas." Brewers violated antitrust laws by using funds for elections, and during Governor Ferguson's impeachment investigators learned that brewers had helped finance his career. When Ferguson ran against William P. Hobby in 1918, Hobby tied Ferguson's loan from the brewers to the German Kaiser, saying that "the breweries and the German-American Alliance were practically the same thing." He trounced Ferguson in the Democratic primaries.

World War I increased women's involvement in the prohibition movement, which led to a law that forbade the sale of alcohol within ten miles of housed troops. Then the state closed saloons. When Congress passed the Eighteenth Amendment in 1920, Texas followed with its own amendment. Illegal stills continued to supply people and speakeasies during the 1920s through underground bootleggers. Galveston's Rum Row became the state's center for smuggling liquor from foreign ports. Powerful politicians failed to support prohibition, and it was eventually repealed during the Depression.

THE DECLINE OF PROGRESSIVISM

Although progressive reforms included women's suffrage and prohibition, America grew more conservative after World War I. People linked sweeping change, which included organized labor and race relations, with the Russian Revolution and communists. In Galveston longshoremen held strikes, causing Governor Hobby to declare martial law and send in Texas Rangers and National Guard troops. The Texas legislature then passed an open-port law which prevented strikes harmful to commerce, thus blunting the open-shop labor market. Several dozen race riots also flared. The most noted in Texas was the Longview Race Riot of 1919 caused by the murder of a black Texan involved with an Anglo woman. Governor Hobby again sent over two hundred guardsmen. When the NAACP national office protested, the governor replied: "Your organization can contribute more to the advancement of both races by keeping your representatives and their propaganda out of this state than in any other way."

As the "teen" years changed to the 1920s, Texans looked around and still saw poverty among tenant farmers, monopolies, and few laws to protect women and children. When former senator Joe Bailey ran for governor against Pat Neff, the first governor to campaign in a car, he made the mistake of opposing everything from prohibition to women's suffrage. Neff swept the election. Voters sought a new kind of reform in a new era with the promise of prosperity.

Chapter XIII

The Business of America Is Business

"There is as much chance of repealing the Eighteenth Amendment as there is for a humming-bird to fly to the planet Mars with the Washington Monument tied to its tail."

—Senator Morris Sheppard

The early 1920s brought prosperity to millions of Americans. As the popular song went, "Life is just a bowl of cherries." The stock market boomed. Factories buzzed. Trade thrived. The population of Texas increased by over a million and oil production soared because of another bonanza strike in the east near Kilgore. Then on October 29, 1929, the stock market crashed and washed away the good times with the loss of forty billion dollars, ushering in the most devastating depression in history that lasted until the beginning of World War II. During the next decade, millions stumbled in the dark, praying for light to once again shine over the U.S.

THE "ROARING TWENTIES"

Flappers, speakeasies, silent films, mobsters, and automobiles all helped shape new cultural values after World War I. Songs such as "Oh, You Great Big Beautiful Doll" and "I Love My Wife, But Oh You Kid," coupled with flashy clothes and rumble-seat sex bewildered many Americans—including conservative Texans who worried about girls wearing makeup, short skirts, and dancing the Charleston. Even black Americans were writing poetry and playing jazz in clubs. What was the country coming to? Ex-Senator Joe Bailey cursed the fox trot and bunny hug, saying he wanted a return to the square dance and songs such as "My Old Kentucky Home." Many mused about the good old days.

President Calvin Coolidge thought "the business of America is business." Part of this country-wide movement also hit the Lone Star state. Houston became the largest city in Texas with a population of nearly 300,000, followed by Dallas and San Antonio. Sixteen Texas cities had populations of at least 25,000. Texans spent $24 million a year on movies and drove a million cars on nearly 19,000 miles of road. They bought everything from record players to washing machines—mostly on the installment plan. Times looked pretty good.

Economic growth spurred such unparalleled change. The 1920s oil boom in Texas furnished 20 percent of the world's oil supply and 40 percent of all gas in the U.S. One promoter bought land for $12,000 and sold it six months later for over a million dollars. Even the University of Texas and Texas A&M University got rich from land donated in the 19th century. Lumber mills, meatpacking plants, and manufacturing increased over 50 percent during this decade which meant more jobs for more people.

Yet shadowy signs appeared during the decade. A postwar recession hit the country in 1921, causing a slump in the stock market and fewer jobs for veterans returning home after the war. National income dropped 28 percent. The government cancelled almost half of its six billion dollars worth of contracts. Even though farm production increased in Texas during the 1920s, profits slid because of surpluses from the war. Cotton lost its kingship, dropping from around forty cents to ten cents a pound. New machinery such as tractors, harvesters, and cultivators not only cost money but did the work of many laborers. Yet many land-owning farmers and tenants saw fewer profits because their debts increased to keep up with technology. Coal and textile industries also plunged.

Although now forgotten, the pre-stock-market era was also a time of unrest, even though President Harding promised a fast return to "normalcy." The Senate's rejection of U.S. membership in the League of Nations increased anxieties. Anything "alien" became suspicious and conspiratorial. The red scare made people wonder if communism would spread through the U.S. as fast as in Russia, Hungary, and Germany, bringing with it strikes and labor protests. Fundamentalist bible thumpers ranted over the teaching of evolution in schools. Prohibition crusaders preached against alcohol, calling America a lost generation. "In this age of cities … temptations about our youth … increase, such as foul pictures, corrupt literature, leprous shows, gambling, slot machines, saloons and Sabbath breaking," exhorted one book, "We are trying to raise saints in hell." All this provided ballast for the rise of the new Ku Klux Klan, which eventually claimed three to five million members nationally in the early 1920s, including several hundred thousand women seduced by appeals to the traditions of home, family, and church.

THE INVISIBLE EMPIRE: THE KNIGHTS OF THE KU KLUX KLAN

The new Ku Klux Klan flourished in Arkansas, Louisiana, Oklahoma, and Texas where it sought to cleanse the Jazz Age of moral and political looseness. It installed the first chapter in Houston calling it Sam Houston Klan No. 1. Word spread and members of the fraternal order eventually reached around 140,000 in Texas, including some prominent and well-educated people. Recruiters (kleagles) played on regional prejudices against Catholics, Jews, blacks, radicals, Mexicans, demon rum, gambling, and immoral women. Its creed attacked anything opposed to white Protestant values. Founder William J. Simmons stated: "Any real man, any native-born white American citizen who is not affiliated with any foreign institution and who loves his country and his flag may become a member of the Ku Klux Klan, whether he lives, north, south, east or west." Although passing itself off as a progressive movement, this conservative order really sought a return to earlier Southern ways, using vigilantism to achieve

The Ku Klux Klan parading in Beaumont, Texas, 1922

its idea of law and order. The El Paso Frontier Klan No. 100, for example, used the city's border proximity to make citizens fearful of bootleggers, crime, and unwanted Mexican laborers. In Houston the KKK reminded people of the 1917 race riot to incite them against black Texans.

For a while, the KKK infiltrated churches and government. Some Protestant ministers praised it because they feared the rise of Roman Catholicism and loss of congregations due to movies, music, and mobility of cars. Before long, the "invisible empire" controlled police departments, juries, and judges. Texas Governor Neff hesitated to denounce the KKK, although newspapers and politicians such as Joseph S. Cullinan and Maury Maverick spoke out. In 1922 the Klan endorsed Earle B. Mayfield for the U.S. Senate from Texas who won over former governor James E. Ferguson. Klansmen and sympathizers also entered the Texas legislature. Then in 1924, the Klan's candidate for governor, Felix D. Robertson, ran against "Ma" Ferguson's bonnet and canned preserves, and lost the election, which helped lead to the movement's demise in Texas.

Eventually, the Klan's violent tactics wore on Texans. Hooded members whipped and tarred and feathered an attorney in Houston who represented black Texan clients. In Dallas they branded the initials KKK on a black bellhop's forehead with acid. They castrated a black dentist who got involved with an Anglo woman. Some Klansmen even fed victims "through rock grinders." The stripping, beating, and tarring and feathering of a young woman in Tenaha helped spur protests nationally against KKK abuses. As one sheriff put it, "I do not consider any organization or association that wears masks, operates in the night, and carries guns to perpetuate their purpose and to prevent their identification law-abiding citizens." Ma Ferguson got the legislature to pass a law making it a criminal offense to wear masks in public, which threw the KKK into a tailspin.

WALL STREET LAYS AN EGG

Many reasons have been given for the great crash of 1929, most focusing on an unstable economy, high tariffs on European goods, and feverish over speculation. One broker recalled: "Wherever one went, one met people who told of their stock-market winnings. At dinner tables, at bridge, on golf links, on trolley cars, in country post offices, in barber chairs, in factories and shops of all kinds." Easy money flowed as investors bought stocks on credit, selling them for better stocks, paying billions in interest. Large companies merged. Brokers grew rich. Then the house of cards col-

Chapter XIII: The Business of America Is Business

Run on San Antonio's City Bank during the Great Depression

lapsed. Within several weeks after the stock market crash, its loss equaled twice the country's debt. Overnight millions of jobs vanished.

President Herbert Hoover, once a respected statesman and humanitarian, played scapegoat for the deepening depression. When elected in 1929, he promised a chicken in every pot and two cars in every garage. Hoover believed in the virtues of individualism, that people should support government and not government support people, the reason why he opposed relief programs during the early Depression. He preached equality of opportunity based on whatever one's "intelligence, character, ability and ambition entitle[d] him" in society. But conditions worsened as production collapsed, millions lost jobs, and banks closed. Hoover introduced a road-building program and tried to cut government costs, an idea that irritated both business and the American people. Even when the New York Federal Reserve Bank cut rates to 2½ percent, the Dow continued to spiral downward as commodities fell to a new low and rye sold for less than sawdust. By 1933 the gross national product dropped from 104.4 billion dollars to 74.2 billion dollars. Farm prices plummeted 61 percent from 1929 to 1933.

Many Texas newspapers and magazines refused to admit a depression existed and wrote positive articles supporting the Hoover administration. What was there to worry about with oil, natural gas, cotton, and the lumber industry? Unemployment rose more slowly in Texas than in the North, taking a while before people began to feel the economic crunch. As one labor weekly said, "What the American farmer would appreciate is more cash and less optimistic conversation." Publications then predicted the depression had hit bottom and would soon end. When conditions failed to improve, the press found things to praise about the crisis: people grew thriftier, more considerate of others, and began to search for solutions.

Hoover became associated with poverty. Empty pants pockets were called "Hoover flags," and park bench newspapers "Hoover blankets." Texans who built shantytowns called them "Hoovervilles." People slept in doorways, packing boxes, and fought over scraps from the garbage cans of restaurants. Even the rich tightened their belts and let servants go. Although Texas governor Ross Sterling agreed with Hoover's views about relief, he failed to solve the unemployment crisis. Crop prices continued to fall: cotton to $.05 a pound, corn and cattle 50 percent lower than in the late 1920s. The Texas legislature passed the Texas Cotton Acreage Control Law, which limited cotton production to 30 percent of a farmer's land. This forced farmers to let tenants go which increased unemployment. The law was soon struck down as unconstitutional. Hamburgers sold for a nickel each and milk for four to five cents a quart—cheap for the employed.

Conditions grew bleak in Texas. Rural areas suffered because much of the state's population depended on the production of cotton, which collapsed in some counties. Eighteen thousand people lost work in Dallas, and both teacher and police salaries were cut in San Antonio. A million people went on government relief. Building slowed to a standstill. Companies and businesses failed. People welcomed odd jobs. Some became drifters, hitching rides on freight trains and begging from house to house, causing many towns to turn their backs out of fear. Around 45,000 transients passed through El Paso during one six-month period, and some days several hundred tramps got off trains in San Antonio. Organizations such as the Red Cross and Salvation Army set up bread lines and soup kitchens. Churches helped with food and clothes. Some people moved from the cities back to farms, where they could at least grow crops, and farmers burned corn for heat because it cost less than firewood. In Lubbock they plowed up the grass lawn of city hall and planted turnips. The Wichita Falls and Fort Worth zoos sold their animals. Houston turned off half its street lights. One town even caught wild rabbits for food. Drought and grasshoppers made things even worse. Dust storms blew across the state, leaving land dry and crops blighted because of cattle overgrazing and thousands of acres of grass used to grow wheat during World War I.

Before the crash, the second oil boom in east Texas had attracted thousands of wildcatters, squatters, and con artists. The field produced more than 41,000,000 barrels of oil with a daily production of nearly 600,000, which brought temporary prosperity to the area. But prices soon dropped to $.15 a barrel, leading Governor Sterling to send National Guardsmen to shut down the field. Some producers sold "hot oil" (using illegal pipelines) to truckers and independent service stations. The Connally Act (named after the Texas senator) banned the transportation of such oil across state lines, although major oilmen still made enormous profits.

Some historians believe Americans stood on the brink of a revolution before the New Deal. Riots broke out in towns. Groups talked about communism, socialism, even fascism. People desperately needed work and weren't concerned with political ideologies. As one Texan put it: "Write or phone if you hear of any relief coming down my way. I am willing to be either a Democrat or Republican for a few weeks if that will help any."

THE NEW DEAL—RELIEF, RECOVERY, AND REFORM

In 1932 the country elected Franklin D. Roosevelt as president, a Democrat whose campaign song was "Happy Days are Here Again." He received nearly 90 percent of the votes in Texas. Texan John Nance Garner became vice president, a key figure among congressmen, and probably the second most influential politician in the capital. His friend, Representative Sam Rayburn, also a Texan, chaired the interstate and Foreign Affairs Committee, leading the president to remark that more Texans were running the government than from any other state. Powerful Texan Jesse H. Jones also chaired the Reconstruction Finance Corporation (RFC), which gave billions in federal funds to states during the 1930s.

Roosevelt kicked off the "New Deal for the forgotten man" in 1933 which the Senate quickly approved by a 73 to 7 vote. Through fresh projects Texas received millions of dollars to build roads, public buildings, parks, and bridges. As Governor James Allred promised: "I'm gonna grab all [the money] I can get for the State of Texas." The WPA (Works Progress Administration) and the PWA (Public Works Administration) gave work to more than 600,000 Texans. These government organizations sponsored the construction of public buildings, parks, and monuments. The San Jacinto Monument, the Riverwalk in San Antonio, and the tower of the Main Building at the University of Texas in Austin all resulted from these programs. The Federal Arts Project (FAP) provided funds for artists to paint, sculpt, and photograph; the Federal Theatre Project (FTP) enabled playwrights to get works staged; and the Federal Writers' Project (FWP) produced guidebooks and recorded documents. The NYA (National Youth Administration) under a young Lyndon B. Johnson used between 10,000 and 18,000 youngsters each month to build playgrounds and roadside parks.

San Jacinto Monument built with New Deal funds. This is the second tallest monument in the U.S. and the world's tallest masonry tower, with a 110-ton star at the top.

Chapter XIII: The Business of America Is Business   161

The 310-foot-high University Tower at the University of Texas in Austin was also built with New Deal funds. It would become infamous in 1966 when an ex-marine shot people randomly from its observation deck.

The New Deal's Agricultural Adjustment Act (AAA) of 1933, designed to help tenant farmers, worked against them because of loopholes. It directed farmers to plow under 10 million acres of cotton in an effort to raise market prices. Landlords evicted tenants rather than share government checks, and threatened complainers. One woman wrote President Roosevelt: "For thirty-nine years myself and husband have farmed, worked from 4:30 a.m. until 9:30 p.m. and ... never in our life have we faced such a time as your administration has thrust upon us. Now with old age creeping upon my husband and I are losing everything."

Mechanization continued to raise unemployment. One tractor did the work of a dozen farm hands. As a result, farmers decreased by 83,000 in Texas during the Depression. Many poor Anglo Texans either went on relief or joined black and Mexican Texan sharecroppers and migrant workers, whom they resented because some large landowners preferred them to Anglos. One case worker wrote: "So it was a case of begging from the government to give you food to bring home to your children. They used to be sitting in a line out in the back yard of our office, a hundred at a time on a Saturday morning ... It just got me, that I could not stand it." Even Roosevelt admitted in 1933 that one-third of the country was ill-fed, ill-clothed, and ill-housed.

Blacks suffered even more than poor Anglos during the Depression. In Boston, almost 33 percent of blacks were unemployed as opposed to 19 percent of white persons. Nearly twice as many skilled blacks were also jobless. Around 35 percent were unemployed in Austin and Houston, often because of discrimination. Most worked as domestic servants and as farm laborers, which denied them benefits such as the new Social Security System. The Depression ruined all but several black Texan banks and insurance companies. Few qualified for loans through the Bankhead-Jones Farm Tenancy Act to buy their own farms. Many would remain sharecroppers and continue to lose representation in government.

Mexican Texans also got hit hard. Many who were illiterate and untrained ended up with low-paying jobs as maids, kitchen helpers, and warehousemen. Around 400,000 became migrant workers, earning about $37.50 for six months labor. Workers in a San Antonio cigar factory walked out, and thousands of pecan shellers went on strike asking for more than four cents a pound. Members of the Sheep Shearer's Union of North America in west Texas also struck. Roosevelt's WPA and NYA offered some help to Mexican Texans but excluded many from programs because they worked in agriculture, were aliens, or didn't understand claim processes. Around a quarter of a million became "repatriates" and returned to Mexico during the Depression.

Some Texans turned to crime as a solution to the problem. Around two thousand homicides a year occurred in the state. Bootleggers cleaned up until the repeal of prohibition in 1935. Others became petty thieves. Gangsters robbed, kidnapped, and killed anyone who got in their way. Rat-faced Clyde Barrow, a fifth-grade dropout, and cold-blooded waitress Bonnie Parker spent several years robbing banks through five states. A posse led by Frank Hamer finally caught up with Bonnie and Clyde in 1934 and riddled their stolen V8 deluxe Ford sedan with bullets.

One bright spot of the Depression in Texas was the Centennial Exposition of 1936, which cost around $25 million and dazzled six million visitors. Opened by Governor James V. Allred with a $50,000 gold key, it sported an Art Deco-Neo-Egyptian style, and housed everything from a reproduction of Judge Roy Bean's Jersey Lily saloon to an entertainment center shaped like an oceanliner. The "Cavalcade of Texas" production featured three hundred performers. Although the exposition lost money, it reopened the next year as the Greater Texas and Pan-American Exposition, attracting millions more.

WORLD WAR II

On December 7, 1941, Japan bombed Pearl Harbor, killing 2,300 servicemen and wounding 1,100 others. The attack sunk most of the U.S. Pacific Fleet and destroyed 150 planes. Both Japan and Germany had already invaded other countries. When England and France entered World War II in 1940, the neutral U.S. passed the draft and Lend-Lease program which sent supplies. After Pearl Harbor, Texas senator Tom Connally introduced the resolution which led to the declaration of war on Japan. Italy and Germany, honoring treaties with Japan, then declared war on the U.S.

Most Americans had expected the war—85 percent in a Gallup Poll study during the summer of 1941. Foreign correspondents felt likewise. But although industrial production had increased 66 percent from 1935-39, and the government had invested $8.3 billion in defense spending, the country remained so unprepared for war that recruits trained with wooden logs and rifles. General George C. Marshall warned that only 600,000 soldiers out of 1,400,000 were ready for combat, and that the country would lose half a million men in a conflict with Germany.

THE WAR FRONT

Texans, for the most part, supported the war effort. Around 750,000 men served—a larger proportion than any other state. Twenty two thousand either died or suffered wounds during the conflict. The state also became a military center, training 1.2 million soldiers at its fifteen army bases and 200,000 others at forty military airfields. Randolph Field continued as the West Point of the Air Force. The national headquarters of the Air Force Training Command was at Carswell Field in Fort Worth. Brooks and Kelly fields and Lackland Air Base also became training centers.

The state contributed its share of leaders and heroes to the war. Dwight D. Eisenhower, Allied Supreme Commander in Europe, was born in Denison, Texas, and Chester Nimitz, Pacific Fleet Admiral, was born in Fredericksburg. Walter Krueger of San Antonio served as commanding general of the Sixth Army, and James Earl Rudder of Eden led the 2nd

Chester Nimitz, U.S. Pacific Fleet Admiral during World War II was born in Fredericksburg, Texas.

Ranger Battalion during the 1944 Normandy invasion. Many Texan soldiers also received honors—thirty-six being awarded the Congressional Medal of Honor. Johnnie Hutchins, who died while saving his ship from a torpedo, received the Medal of Honor, and the navy named the USS *Johnnie Hutchins* after him. Dorie (Doris) Miller, a black mess man on a battleship during the attack on Pearl Harbor, received the Navy Cross for manning an antiaircraft gun and shooting down several Japanese planes. Another black, Roy Harmon, received the Navy Cross and a ship, the USS *Harmon*, was named after him for dying while trying to save a shipmate. Macario Garcia destroyed two nests of German machine guns singlehandedly and won the Medal of Honor. Four other Mexican Texans also won the Medal of Honor. The two most decorated servicemen from Texas during World War II were Samuel Dealey, a submarine commander who sank sixteen Japanese ships, and Lieutenant Audie Murphy of Farmerville, who killed fifty Germans under fire. When headquarters asked how close the Germans were, Murphy replied: "If you'll just hold the phone, I'll let you talk to one of the bastards!" Murphy later became a movie star and played himself in *To Hell and Back*.

The Thirty-Sixth United States Infantry Division from Texas also distinguished itself. The Second Battalion of the 131st Field Artillery unit, known as the Lost Battalion, surrendered to the Japanese during the battle of Java and vanished for over a year. Many labored on a railroad from Burma to Bangkok, Thailand, which included a bridge later celebrated in the book and film *The Bridge on the River Kwai*. Other units of the division fought in the attack on Salerno, Sicily, in the capture of Rome in 1944, and during the occupation of Germany in 1945.

Around twelve thousand Texan women also served during World War II, doing everything from being military nurses with the American Red Cross to joining the new Women's Air Force Service Pilots. The most distinguished was Oveta Culp Hobby, wife of the former Texas governor. As director of the new Women's Army Auxiliary Corps, she increased its numbers to 100,000 and received the Distinguished Service Medal. Colonel Hobby once remarked: "It's not just the combat forces we need … Total war means everybody is involved in the struggle." In 1953 President Eisenhower appointed her chairman of the Federal Security Agency.

THE HOME FRONT

During the war, Texans tightened their belts and made sacrifices like the rest of Americans. Many shortages required rationing. Nearly all of the country's crude rubber supply had been lost to Japanese invasions in the Far East, leaving only small stockpiled amounts. The government froze tire production and began to experiment with synthetic rubber plants, asking for old beach balls, overshoes, and hot-water bottles. Gas rationing followed as the government banned pleasure driving and passed a 35-mile-per-hour speed limit on the country's highways. Pipe-smoking Texas Governor Coke R. Stevenson ("Calculatin' Coke") opposed this because of the state's size, calling gas as necessary to the state as the saddle, rifle, and bible. People used trains, buses, bicycles. Meanwhile, a pipeline known as the Big Inch was built between Texas oilfields and the northeastern states, which eventually pumped 300,000 barrels of oil a day to east coast refineries. A second pipeline called The Little Inch followed which also carried gasoline from Texas to the east coast. Food rationing hit the hardest, limiting the consumption of sugar, coffee, and meat. Homemakers saved kitchen fats, tin cans, razor blades, nylon stockings, and empty lipstick tubes. Even buttons, needles, and bobby pins became scarce. The government urged: "Use it up, wear it out, make it do or do without."

World War II ended the Depression in Texas. Military posts alone brought millions into the state. Industry expanded. The Gulf Coast near Houston became the world's largest producer of petrochemicals. Steel mills operated at full capacity. Texas City held the world's largest tin smelter. The need for paper and lumber renewed the east Texas woodpulp business. Aircraft factories opened in the Dallas-Fort Worth area and shipyards from Galveston to Corpus Christi needed thousands of workers, causing many to move from rural to urban centers. Women also entered the work force on assembly lines in plants, many remaining there after the war's end. Manufacturing expanded a whopping five times.

Bring the Boys Home

On April 12, 1945, President Roosevelt died of a cerebral hemorrhage. Harry S. Truman became president one month before Berlin fell and Germany surrendered. Eyes turned towards the Pacific War, where the U.S. finally took Iwo Jima after suffering thousands of casualties and Joe Rosenthal's flag-raising photo became famous and appeared in numerous papers. (One Marine in it, Harlon Block, came from Yorktown, Texas.) Then the U.S. dropped two atomic bombs on the Japanese cities of Hiroshima and Nagasaki. This led to Japan's surrender in August 1945.

The war was over! Two million people gathered in New York's Times Square as five thousand tons of confetti fell onto the streets. From San Antonio to Santa Barbara and Syracuse, the country celebrated—dancing, singing, cheering, and all saying, "Bring the boys home!" During those four war-torn years, a new Texas had emerged—from a predominantly rural culture to a more refined, urban one. Many now asked: What would happen in the postwar years as expansion began to unwind? What would happen to all the jobs, the prosperity, the New Deal programs for the poor? They would soon find out.

Chapter XIV

Gone To Texas

"We're just common folks."—Governor Preston Smith

Following World War II, Texas entered into a period of rapid growth that left behind the wild-west Hollywood image of gunslingers, Indians, and country places like in the movie *The Best Little Whorehouse in Texas*. Chemicals, electronics, and agribusiness made the difference. By 1973 the state included over fourteen thousand manufacturing plants. Farms and farm tenancy decreased because of mechanization. Livestock sales spiraled with the help of feedlots. Even the population reached over eleven million, moving the state from sixth to fourth largest in the country.

BOOM AND BUST

The period between 1945 and 1982 carved a Texas renaissance of sorts. The University of Texas and Texas A&M became world-class institutions. The state also added two dozen other four-year universities, nearly fifty community colleges, and seven medical schools. This didn't include around three dozen private colleges. Student enrollment reached 762,000 by 1986. The arts sprouted wings. Skylines pierced the skies. And San Antonio hosted the 1968 HemisFair as part of its 150th anniversary. (The Tower of the Americas still stands from this fair with a revolving restaurant at the top.) The Houston Astrodome, constructed in 1965, cost $45 million and became the largest air-conditioned domed sports arena in the world with seating for forty-five thousand baseball fans and fifty-two thousand football buffs.

Texas was on a roll—yet it remained a jumble of contradictions. Outsiders still controlled much of its wealth, especially eastern investors earlier politicians had tried to keep out. These included such economic giants as Humble Oil and Refining Company, DuPont, and U.S. Steel. Senator Wilbert (Pappy) Lee O'Daniel called Texas "New York's most valuable foreign possession." John Gunther mused in *Inside U.S.A.*: "Texas reminded me a good deal of Argentina … cattle culture, absentee ownership, vast land holdings by semi-feudal barons, a great preoccupation with weather, an under-developed middle class, interminable flatness and open spaces, and fierce political partisanship and nationalism."

SCOUNDRELS AND SKIRMISHES

Texas had its share of controversies during this period. In 1945, Herman Sweatt took legal action when the University of Texas law school denied him entrance and won, a victory that opened doors for other blacks to attend graduate schools. Another noted controversy involved Baptist preacher Homer Price Rainey's clash at the University of Texas. Appointed president of the university in 1939, Rainey locked horns with the Board of Regents over the firing of faculty, the rejection of research funds, and the banning of John Dos Passos's *U.S.A.* Rainey ended up fired, hosted a radio show, and then ran for governor in 1946. He was beaten by Beauford Jester, who called himself "the only candidate in the race who can go to the governor's chair without mud and slime and filth on his hands."

Such scandals caught the public's eye. One of the earliest involved the insurance business. Many of the thirteen hundred companies chartered during the early 1950s collapsed and policyowners lost millions. A Board of Insurance Commissioners began to regulate these companies, rating policies, monitoring agents, and requiring a minimum capitalization of $250,000. But bankruptcies continued. When the U.S. Trust and Guaranty failed, it owned five times more in claims than its reserves, and an executive fled to Brazil with a fortune. An investigation found that the state's insurance commissioner had accepted gifts.

The "grandpappy of all Texas scandals" involved State Land Commissioner Bascom Giles, who tried to cheat veterans out of millions of dollars through the Veteran's Land Program after World War II. Among other things, he chose dishonest appraisers and approved inflated prices for land owned by nonexistent veterans. He received a prison sentence, the first elected state official ever indicted while in office, and earned Kenneth Towery of the *Cuero Record* a Pulitzer Prize for exposing the underhanded plot.

Chapter XIV: Gone To Texas

The Sharpstown scandal in the early 1970s involved a spate of politicians, causing a legislature housecleaning by candidates with the slogan, "throw the rascals out." Businessman Frank W. Sharp hatched a complicated stock-fraud scheme that involved the Sharpstown State Bank and the National Bankers Life Insurance Companies, both of which he owned. State officials involved included profiteer Texas House Speaker Gus Mutscher and possibly Governor Preston Smith. Sharp succeeded in getting bank-deposit insurance bills passed, saying they would help the little banks. But the Federal Securities and Trade Commission (SEC) filed charges and Mutscher, along with two others, was convicted of conspiracy and given five years probation, thanks to the vigilance of a group called the Dirty 30. Mutscher later admitted contriving the scheme to "make money for all of us—what other reason could there be?"

The rights of coastal states to exploit off-shore oil became the century's most sensational debate between states and the federal government. In 1947 the United States Supreme Court held that "California is not the owner of the three-mile marginal belt along its coast, and that the Federal Government rather than the state has paramount rights in and power over that belt, an incident to which is full dominion over the resources of the soil under that water area, including oil." Three years later, they applied the same ruling to Texas and Louisiana. It outraged Texans who claimed oil rights up to ten and a half miles offshore because of their earlier stature as a republic instead of a territory. In 1837 President Andrew Jackson and the United States Senate both had recognized this boundary. So had Mexico in the Treaty of Guadalupe Hidalgo in 1848 and the Gadsden Treaty in 1853. President Harry S. Truman, however, vetoed efforts to protect Texas rights to offshore oil. U.S. Representative Sam Rayburn, who first sided with the federal government, later presented the Rayburn Plan, which gave Louisiana, Texas, and California rights to two-thirds of oil within the ten-mile limit and one-third beyond. Although supported by Governor Allan Shivers, Attorney General Price Daniel swayed public opinion against it. The Supreme Court supported federal ownership of all submerged lands off the U.S. coast. When Dwight D. Eisenhower ran for president in 1952, he needed Texas's support and promised to support the tidelands legislation, leading Texas to endorse a Republican candidate instead of a Democrat. When Ike signed the bill, he asked: "Where's Texas?"

Two Texas Democrats played key roles in Eisenhower's election—Sam Rayburn (elected two dozen times to the House of Representatives) and his protégé Lyndon B. Johnson. Both politicians were influenced by John

Nance "Cactus Jack" Garner and Franklin D. Roosevelt. Rayburn ("Mr. Sam") served as minority leader, majority leader, and Speaker of the House of Representatives, and is considered by some the House's best orator in U.S. history. Many of his boosters wanted him to run for president in 1952.

Lyndon B. Johnson, who often started speeches with "from Sam Houston to Sam Rayburn," was like Texas—a bundle of contradictions. A former schoolteacher at Sam Houston High School, he became friends with Rayburn, who landed him a position as Director of the National Youth Administration during Roosevelt's New Deal. He got elected to the U.S. House of Representatives in 1937 and became a U.S. senator in 1948, stumping in a helicopter called the Johnson City Windmill. Before long, he became minority leader and then majority leader under Eisenhower and also acquired a fortune through radio and TV stations in Texas. During these years, Johnson opposed Republican senator Joseph McCarthy's "witch hunts" for communists, and supported the Civil Rights Act of 1957 and the National Aeronautic and Space Administration (NASA) bill.

In the 1960 presidential election, Senator John F. Kennedy chose Johnson as his running mate, which both parties opposed, but Kennedy needed the Southern vote and a conservative to balance his liberal views. He beat Richard Nixon in a close election and took Texas with fewer than fifty thousand votes. On November 22, 1963, President Kennedy was assassinated in Dallas, and Johnson became president. He later said, "I became President. But for millions of Americans I was still illegitimate, a naked man with no presidential covering, a pretender to the throne, an illegal usurper. And then there was Texas, my home, the home of both the murder and the murder of the murderer." Yet Johnson managed to get many of Kennedy's programs that related to taxes, civil rights, and poverty passed through Congress. Johnson was reelected in 1964 after beating Barry Goldwater with emotionally charged TV spots, bumper stickers such as "In your gut, you know he's nuts," and other clever campaigns tactics which led many voters to believe Goldwater "would act without thinking." Johnson carried one of the biggest popular votes in U.S. history and an Electoral College margin second only to the 1936 election of Franklin Roosevelt. But the war in Vietnam overshadowed his political successes, and he declined to run again in 1968.

During Johnson's years as vice president and president, Texas Democrats tried to halt the growing power of Republicans in the state. Their champion became John B. Connally, Johnson's political manager and secretary of the navy who became governor by a narrow margin in 1962.

Chapter XIV: Gone To Texas

President Lyndon B. Johnson in the oval office at the White House

Connally gained national recognition after being shot during Kennedy's assassination and served as governor until 1969. He then became President Nixon's secretary of the treasury, and after Vice President Spiro Agnew's resignation was named as Nixon's choice for vice president, which caused protest in the Senate because of his image as a wheeler dealer. The same happened when he sought the Republican nomination for president in 1980. When the Texas oil boom busted in the 1980s, Connally declared bankruptcy because of investment losses.

Few expected the Texas oil bust, which also ruined other millionaires. The oil industry, which involved 25 percent of the state's goods and services, was three times greater than agriculture. Like in the 1920s, people believed good times would never end and failed to notice falling figures for crude oil, which had skyrocketed from $3.18 in 1970 to $39 in 1981, but then slipped to a low of $10 in 1986. The result? A Texas depression in the year it celebrated the Sesquicentennial of the Republic of Texas. Real-estate prices plunged. Banks closed (50 in 1987 and 113 in 1988). Companies such as Exxon and Chevron slashed drilling and exploration. Nearly a million workers lost their jobs. Unemployment ran as high as 17 percent in the Rio Grande Valley. Even oil stocks tumbled. One joke ran: "How do you get a Texas oil man out of a tree?" The answer was "Cut the rope."

THE GREAT TEXAS TURNAROUND

Things looked dreary for a while—but it's hard to keep Texans down for long. Although oil production slumped from 700 million barrels in 1988 to less than 400 million barrels in 2000, black gold still brought in $20 billion dollars a year. Agricultural products such as cattle, cotton, and sheep continued to expand and earn another $14 billion a year. Then Gruman moved to Houston and J.C. Penney to Plano, Southwestern Bell bought Metromedia, IBM built in the Dallas/Fort Worth area. Other companies such as Motorola, Tandy, and Texas Instruments also expanded facilities. Electronic giant Sematech chose Austin for its new headquarters. Although Congress killed the plans to build a Superconducting Super Collider (SSC) in Waxahachie, the project brought other businesses such as GTE and Fujitsu to the state. Foreign trade with Mexico also mushroomed with the North American Free Trade Agreement (NAFTA). And consumer services soared. San Antonio, with its enormous tourist trade, even built a new Alamodome.

The decade's biggest news? Texan George H. W. Bush was elected president in 1992—which meant more Texans in Washington, D.C., again.

CHAPTER XIV: Gone To Texas

President George H. W. Bush

The former head of the Central Intelligence Agency (CIA), Bush had been elected vice president in 1980 and reelected in 1984. He also served as ambassador to the United Nations. His son, George W. Bush would later carry on the family political tradition and serve two terms as president.

Today problems remain in Texas: poverty, education, water, taxes, and environmental concerns over pollution. But racial integration, so controversial during the 1950s, had greatly improved. The condition of Mexican Texans has also advanced as their presence and political clout continue to grow. Texas now has the country's second largest Hispanic population, which could become a majority by 2030. (It's already the majority in San Antonio.) Influential Mexican Texans include Representative Henry B. Gonzalez, who chaired the influential House Banking Committee. He once made the incisive remark: "I believe in the Constitution—and in groceries too." Dan Morales became state attorney general. Henry B. Cisneros was elected the youngest councilman in San Antonio's history, carrying more Anglo votes than Mexican Texan ones, then served as mayor of San Antonio and as U.S. secretary of Housing and Urban Development in the Clinton administration. In 2001 Ed Garza became San Antonio's second Mexican Texan mayor. Middle-class Mexican, black, and Anglo Texans now see eye to eye on more issues, which will improve communities and provide what writer Herman Gallegos called "a better life for the many and not just the good life for the few."

Statue of Paisano Pete in Fort Stockton, Texas

Author Marco Portales talks about race issues in *Latino Sun Rising*: "People need to recognize that race and skin color affect the nature of our experiences. Historically, race divided people. Race now needs to unite us. Instead of legally asserting that race is illusory, we ought to embrace our human qualities and traits, excluding only what harms others." He quotes from J. Hector St. John de Crevecoeur's *What is an American* (1782): "Here individuals of all nations are melted into a new race of men."

Women have also played active roles in modern Texas culture and politics. President Lyndon B. Johnson promoted black Texan Barbara Jordan's career. She first secured a seat in the Texas senate, then moved to the U.S. House of Representatives gaining respect during the 1974 Watergate hearings, and finally became the first woman to keynote a Democratic National Convention in 1976. Liz Carpenter, press secretary to President Johnson, formed the Texas Women's Political Caucus. Lila Cockrell was elected mayor of San Antonio in 1975. Black Texans Eddie Bernice Johnson and Senfronia Thompson as well as Mexican Texan Irma Rangel were elected as state representatives. And in 1990, flamboyant Ann Richards won the governorship. Her first 650 appointments were 48 percent female, 25 percent Hispanic, and 12 percent black. She said that "it is the right thing to do … it is the smart thing to do."

CHAPTER XIV: Gone To Texas

A view of the city of San Antonio from King William district

View of the Houston skyline

LONE STAR SHINING

So where does the Lone Star state stand as a modern cultural and industrial state? Have the "gone to Texas" signs been torn down? Is it mostly folklore, like Pecos Bill and cowboys on the cattle trail? Or was John Steinbeck right when he observed: "Texas is a state of mind, but I think it is more than that. It is a mystique closely approaching a religion."

The state's population is now around 26,000,000. People keep pouring in, not only from the South but also from the Northeast to start new lives, as did early settlers. They like the Sunbelt climate, economic growth, and cheap real estate, although costs continue to rise.

Texas is the only state with three cities that boast populations exceeding one million: Houston, San Antonio, and Dallas. They rank among the country's top ten.

The state's gross product of $1.09 trillion is second highest next to California. Thirty-three billionaires call Texas "home." It also has more Fortune 500 companies than any other state and exports more merchandise. There are twenty-six refineries in Texas, which make up one-fourth of the U.S.'s refining capacity. The Exxon-Mobile Corporation's plant outside of Houston is the nation's largest oil refinery. Dow Chemical is also north of Corpus Christi.

The Globalization and World Cities Study ranked Dallas and Houston as two of eleven U.S. world-class cities. Only New York City eclipses Houston's theater district. It's also one of five cities in the U.S. with permanent professional resident companies: the Houston Symphony Orchestra, the Houston Ballet, the Houston Grand Opera, and the Alley Theatre. Houston's Texas Medical Center remains the world's largest group of research and healthcare institutions. Its port is the busiest in the U.S.

Texas claims the most airports of any state. The Dallas-Fort Worth International Airport, largest in the state, is also the second largest in the U.S. and fourth largest in the world.

The bottom line? Texas has come a long way since the time when President Sam Houston of the Republic of Texas could only find $200 in the government's coffers. It seems the sky's the limit. Wasn't "Houston" the first word spoken on the moon?

Giant cowboy boots at North Star Mall in San Antonio, Texas

Suggestions for Further Reading

Alexander, Charles C. *The Ku Klux Klan in the Southwest*. Norman: University of Oklahoma Press, 1995.
Anderson, Gary. *The Conquest of Texas*. Norman, OK: University of Oklahoma Press, 2005.
Arreola, Daniel D. *Tejano South Texas*. Austin: University of Texas Press, 2002.
Barker, Eugene. *Stephen F. Austin: Founder of Texas, 1793-1836*. Austin: University of Texas Press, 1926.
Barkley, Roy R. & Mark F. Odintz, eds. *The Portable Handbook of Texas*. Austin: The Texas State Historical Association. 2000.
Barr Allyn. *The African Texans*. College Station, TX: Texas A&M University Press, 2004.
Bradle, William R. *Goliad: The Other Alamo*. Grena, LA: Pelican, 2007.
Branch E. Douglas. *The Hunting of the Buffalo*. Lincoln: University of Nebraska Press, 1997.
Brown, Gary. *James Walker Fannin*. Plano, TX: Republic of Texas Press, 2002.
Brands, H. W. *Lone Star Nation*. New York: Doubleday, 2004.
Campbell, Randolph B. *Gone to Texas*. New York: Oxford University Press, 2003.
Cantrel, Gregg. *Stephen F. Austin: Empressario of Texas*. New Haven, CT: Yale University Press, 1999.
Castenada, Carlos E. *The Mexican Side of the Texas Revolution*. New York: Arno Press, 1976.
Chapa, Juan Bautista. *Texas & Northeastern Mexico, 1630-1690*. Austin: University of Texas Press, 1997.
Chapman, Donald E. and Harriett Denise Joseph. *Explorers and Settlers of Spanish Texas*. Austin: University of Texas Press, 2001.
—. *Spanish Texas, 1519-1821*. Austin: University of Texas Press, 1992.
Christensen, Carol and Thomas Christensen. *The U.S. Mexican War*. San Francisco, CA: Bay Books, 1998.
Cottrell, Steve. *Civil War in Texas and New Mexico Territory*. Gretna, LA: Pelican, 1998.
Crouch, Barry A. *The Freedman's Bureau and Black Texans*. Austin: University of Texas Press, 1992.
Davis, William C. *Lone Star Rising*. New York: Free Press, 2004.

DeLeon, Arnoldo. *Mexican Americans in Texas: A Brief History*. Wheeling, IL: Harlan Davidson, 1999.

Dimmick, Gregg G. *Sea of Mud*. Austin: Texas State Historical Association, 2004.

Dobie, J. Frank. *The Longhorns*. Boston: Little Brown & Company, 1941.

Durham, Merle. *The Lone Star State Divided*. Dallas: Hendrick-Long, 1994.

Eisenhower, John S. D. *So Far from God: The U.S. War with Mexico, 1846-1848*. Norman: University of Oklahoma Press, 1989.

Fehrenbach, T. R. *Comanches*. New York: Anchor Books, 1974.

—. *Lone Star: A History of Texas and the Texans*. New York: Da Capo Press, 2000.

Fisher, Lewis F. *The Spanish Missions of San Antonio*. San Antonio: Maverick, 1998.

Ford, John Salmon. *Rip Ford's Texas*. Austin: University of Texas Press, 1963.

Geron, Kim. *Latino Political Power*. Boulder, CO: Lynne Rienner, 2005.

Goodwyn, Lawrence. *The Populist Movement*. New York: Oxford University Press, 1978.

Graham, Don. *Kings of Texas*. New York: John Wiley & Sons, 2003.

Guthrie, Keith. *Raw Frontier: Armed Conflict Along the Texas Coastal Bend*. Austin: Eakin Press, 1998.

Haley, James L. *Passionate Nation*. New York: Free Press, 2006.

—. *Texas: From Spindletop Through World War II*. New York: St. Martin's Press, 1993.

Hardin, Stephen L. *Texas Iliad*. Austin: University of Texas Press, 1994.

Henderson, Timothy J. *A Glorious Defeat: Mexico and Its War with the United States*. New York: Hill & Wang, 2007.

Hoebel, Ernest Wallace and E. Adamson. *The Comanches*. Norman: University of Oklahoma Press, 1952.

Kownslar, Allan O. *The European Texans*. College Station, TX: Texas A & M University Press, 2004.

Larson, Erik. *Isaac's Storm*. New York: Crown Publishers, 1999.

La Vere, David. *The Texas Indians*. College Station, TX: Texas A & M University Press, 2004.

Linsley, Judith Walker, Ellen Walker Rienstra and Jo Ann Stiles. *Giant Under The Hill: A History of the Spindletop Oil Discovery*. Austin: Texas State Historical Association, 2002.

Libura, Krystyna M., et al. *Echoes of the Mexican-American War*. Berkeley, CA: Groundwood Books, 2004.

Marquis, James. *The Raven: A Biography of Sam Houston*. Austin: University of Texas Press, 2004.

Meier, Matt S. and Felliciano Ribera. *Mexican Americans/American Mexicans*. New York: Hill & Wang, 1993.

Montejano, David. *Anglos and Mexicans in the Making of Texas, 1836-1986.* Austin: University of Texas Press, 1987.

Moore, Stephen L. *Eighteen Minutes.* Dallas: Republic of Texas Press, 2004.

Newcomb, W. W., Jr. *The Indians of Texas: From Prehistoric to Modern Times.* Austin: University of Texas Press, 1961.

Roberts, Randy and James S. Olson. *A Line in the Sand.* New York: Simon & Schuster, 2001.

Simons, Helen and Cathryn A. Hoyt. *Hispanic Texas: A Historical Guide.* Austin: University of Texas Press, 1992.

Smallwood, James M., Barry A. Crouch, and Larry Peacock. *Murder and Mayhem: The War of Reconstruction in Texas.* College Station, TX: Texas A&M University Press, 2003.

Steen, Ralph W. *History of Texas.* Austin: The Steck Company, 1939.

Stout, Jay A. *Slaughter at Goliad.* College Station, TX: Texas A&M University Press, 1985.

Tinkle, Lon. *13 Days to Glory.* College Station, TX: Texas A&M University Press, 1985.

Utley, Robert M. *Lone Star Justice: The First Century of the Texas Rangers.* New York: Oxford University Press, 2002.

Webb, Walter Prescott. *The Texas Rangers: A Century of Frontier Defense.* Austin: University of Texas Press, 2005.

Wooster, Ralph A. *Texas and Texans in the Civil War.* Austin: Eakin Press, 1995.

Photo Credits

Chapter I
page 2: Courtesy of Chase A. Fountain
page 6: Courtesy of Eric Leonard

Chapter II
page 11: Texas Beyond History
page 12: Author
page 13: Author
page 16: Author

Chapter III
page 27: The Daughters of the Republic of Texas Library, San Antonio
page 30: The Granger Collection, New York

Chapter IV
page 34: Center for American History, University of Texas at Austin
page 38: Texas State Library and Archives Commission, Austin
page 40: D.W.C. Baker, *A Texas Scrapbook* (1836)
page 41: E.G. Littlejohn, *Texas History Stories* (1901)
page 42: Library of Congress
page 43: The Daughters of the Republic of Texas Library, San Antonio
page 45: Author
page 46: The Collection of the Dallas Historical Society
page 48: The San Jacinto Museum of History, Houston
page 50: Library of Congress

Chapter V
page 56: J.W. Wilbarger, *Indian Depredations in Texas* (1889)
page 57: Mary M. Brown, *A School History of Texas* (1894)
page 60: Museum of Fine Arts, Houston, The Hogg Brothers Collection, gift of Miss Ima Hogg

Chapter VI
page 64: Library of Congress
page 65: UTSA's Institute of Texan Cultures, San Antonio #073-1316
page 66: N.C. Brooks, *A Complete History of the Mexican War* (1849)
page 68 (top & bottom): Library of Congress
page 69: Amos Carter Museum, Dallas

Chapter VII
page 79: From the collection of the Dallas Historical Society
page 82: From the collection of the Dallas Historical Society
page 83: UTSA's Institute of Texan Cultures, San Antonio, #072-0328
page 90: The University of Texas at Brownsville and Texas Southmost College

Chapter VIII
page 92: UTSA's Institute of Texas Cultures, San Antonio, #073-1476
page 94: Catholic Archives of Texas, Austin

Chapter IX
page 99: Panhandle Plains Historical Museum Research Center, Canyon, Texas
page 100: Colorado Historical Society, Denver
page 102: Library of Congress
page 106: S. Compton Smith, *Chili Con Carne* (1857)
page 108: Amos Carter Museum, Dallas

Chapter X
page 114 (top): Midland County Historical Society, Midland Texas
page 114 (bottom): Rosenberg Library, Galveston
page 119: Author
page 121: Texas State Library and Archives Commission
page 124: Author

Chapter XI
page 126: Texas Energy Museum
page 128: Texas Energy Museum
page 130: Witte Museum, San Antonio
page 133: Houston Public Library

Chapter XII
page 142: Bell County Museum, gift of Mr. and Mrs. James Watt, 1991
page 144: Western History Collection, University of Oklahoma Library
page 145: Arizona Historical Society, Tucson
page 146: Author
page 150: Ora McMullen Room, Kurth Memorial Library, Lufkin, Texas

Chapter XIII
page 155: Houston Metropolitan Research Center, Houston Public Library, Houston
page 157: UTSA's Institute of Texan Cultures, San Antonio, #L-1302-H
page 160: Author
page 161: Author
page 164: Official U.S. Navy photograph

Chapter XIV
page 171: LBJ Library, photo by Yoichi Okamoto
page 173: George Bush Presidential Library
page 174: Fort Stockton City Manager
page 175: Author
page 176: Author
page 178: Author

Index

Abilene, Kansas, 98-99
Adams-Onís Treaty, 4-5, 20
agriculture, 71, 158, 161-162, 172
   cotton, 117-118, 158
   labor organizations for, 118-120
Alamo, the, 12, 14-15, 94
   battle at, 37-43
Allred, Governor James V., 159, 162
annexation of Texas with U.S., 61-62
Apaches, 18-9
archeological finds, 9
Archive War, 59
Austin (city), 57, 59, 70, 123
Austin, Moses, 24-25
Austin, Stephen Fuller, 24, 25, 26-28, 29, 30-31, 32-33, 35, 54, 106

Bailey, Senator Joe, 151, 153-154
barbed wire, 100-101
Bass, Sam, 110
Bean, Judge Roy, 115
Beaumont, 127-129
Béxar. *See* San Antonio
Black Texans, 134-135, 162
Blanton, Annie Webb, 148, 149
Bowie, Colonel James, 35-36, 38, 40, 41, 43
Bradburn, Juan Davis, 29
Brownsville, 83-84, 88
buffalo, 107-110
Burnet, David G., 36, 44, 53, 54, 58
Bush, President George H. W., 172-173

Caddos (Indian tribe), 9, 11, 12

Campbell, Governor Thomas M., 141
Carson, Colonel Christopher "Kit", 80
cattle driving/ranching, 97-103
   fencing problems, 100-102
   and sheep herders, 101
Centennial Exposition of 1936, 162-163
Cherokees, 32, 56-57
Chief Quanah Parker, 105
Chief Santana (Comanche), 104
Childress, George C., 44
Civil War
   blockades and blockade running, 87-89
   Brownsville battle, 83-84
   civilian life during, 84-87, 89
   effect on cattle raising of, 98
   end of, 89-90
   Galveston Bay, battle of, 81-82
   Indian problems during, 79-80
   New Mexico Campaign, 80-81
   Palmito Ranch, battle of, 89-90
   post-Civil War life, 91-
   pro-Union element, 86-87
   Red River campaign, 83-84
   Sabine Pass, battle of, 82-83
   start of, 75, 77-79
   Texas's secession from Union, 77, 78-79
Coahuiltecans, 14, 17
Coke, Richard, 96
Coleto, Battle of, 46-47
Colquitt, Governor Oscar Branch, 141, 145

Comanches, 18-19, 32, 56-57, 58, 93
Compromise of 1850, 7
Concepción, Battle of, 15
Concepción, Mission, 15
Connally, Governor John B., 170-171
Connally, Senator Tom, 163
Consultation, the, 32-33, 36-37
Convention of 1836, 43-44
Corpus Christi de las Isleta, 10
cowboys. *See* cattle driving/ranching
Crockett, Davy, 41, 42
Cunningham, Minnie Fisher, 148

Dallas, 131, 154
Davis, Edmund J., 86, 95-96
de León, Alonso, 11
Depression, the Great, 153, 156-163
Dewitt, Green, 25

early inhabitants, 9-10
education, 57, 73-74, 96, 124, 134, 149, 167
Education Act of 1839, 57
Edwards, Benjamin and Haden, 26
Eisenhower, Dwight D., 163, 169
entertainment and arts, 74, 135
Espada, Mission, 17
ethnic groups, 134-138
explorers (early), 10

Fannin, James W., 35-36, 39, 44, 45, 46-47
Farmers' Alliance, 118, 120, 122
farming. *See* agriculture
Ferguson, Governor James "Pa", 141-143, 150
Ferguson, Governor Miriam "Ma", 142-143, 156
filibusters, 19-21
Fisher, Colonel William S. 59-60
flag of Texas, 61-62
Ford, John S. "Rip", 83-84, 89, 90
Fort Worth, 131
Fredonia, Republic of, 26

Fredonian Rebellion, 26
Freedmen's Bureau, 93
French settlers, 11, 12

Galveston, 81-82, 131-132, 150
Garner, John Nance, 159, 170
Giles, Bascom, 168
Goliad (La Bahia), 45
Goliad massacre, 47
Gonzales, 25
Gould, Jay, 115
Grange, the National, 118, 119
Granger, General Gordon, 92
Grant, James, 44
Greenbackers, the, 118, 120
Guitérrez, Bernardo de Lara, 20-21

Hamilton, Andrew J., 86, 93
Hardin, John Wesley, 110-111
Henderson, James Pinkney, 54, 66
Hertzberg, Anna, 149
Higgins, Patillo, 127
Hobby, Governor William P., 150, 151
Hobby, Oveta Culp, 165
Hogg, Governor James Stephen, 120-122, 127, 135
Homestead Act of 1839, 57
Hoover, President Herbert, 157-158
House, E. M., 139-140
Houston (city), 70, 74, 133, 154, 167, 176, 177
Houston, Sam, 31, 36, 37, 38, 39, 44, 45, 48, 49, 51-52, 54, 58-59, 60, 70, 71, 74, 77, 78-79
Houston Astrodome, 167
Huntington, Collis P., 115

Idar, Jovita, 149
Indian Appropriation Act (1869), 104
Indians, 9-10, 70, 79-80, 103-110
    Apaches, 18-19, 105-106
    and buffalo, 108-110
    Caddos, 9, 11, 12

Cherokees, 32, 56-57
Coahuiltecans, 14, 17
Comanches, 18-19, 32, 56-57, 58, 79-80, 93, 104-105, 106-107
Karankawas, 11, 28
Kickapoos, 80
Kiowa, 104-105
Pueblos, 10-11
Spanish settlers and, 10
Texas Rangers and, 106-107
Tonkawas, 28, 32
U.S. Army and, 103-106
Wichitas, 32
industry, 71, 87, 154, 159, 165-166, 167, 172, 176-177
  in cities, 130, 131
  lumber, 116
  mining, 115-116
  oil, 125-129, 154, 158-159, 165, 172
  and unions, 116-117
Iturbide, Colonel Augustin de, 23

Jester, Governor Beauford, 168
Johnson, Frank, 44
Johnson, Lyndon B., 159, 169, 170, 171
Jones, Dr. Anson, 61
Jones, Jesse H., 159
Jordan, Barbara, 174
Juneteenth, 92, 135

Karankawas (Indian tribe), 11
Kearny, Stephen W., 67
Kenedy, Mifflin, 97
Kholberg, Olga, 149
King, Richard, 73, 97
King Ranch, 97
Kirby, John Henry, 116
Ku Klux Klan, 93, 135, 143, 155-156

Lamar, Mirabeau B., 54-58
Lanham, Governor S.W.T., 140

LaSalle, Rene-Robert (explorer), 11
Law of April 6, 1830, 29
Léon, Martin de, 25
Long, James (filibuster), 20, 21
Long, Jane, 25
Lucas, Anthony, 127, 129

Mackenzie, Ronald S., 105
Magruder, John B., 81-82, 89, 90
Martinez, Governor Antonio, 24
Massanet, Damián, 11
Matamoros, Mexico, 88
McCoy, Joseph G., 98-99
McCullough, Ben, 79
Mexican border clashes, 29-30, 32-33, 144-145
Mexican Revolution (1821), 23-24
Mexican Texans, 135-137, 162, 173
Mexican War of 1846, 6, 63-69
Mier Expedition, 59-60
military posts, 143, 147, 163
missions, 11-12, 14, 17-19
  Concepción, 15
  Espada, 17
  San Antonio de Valero (the Alamo), 12-13, 14-15
  San José, 15, 16
  San Juan, 17
  San Sába, 18
Murphy, Audie, 164
Murrah, Governor Pendleton, 89, 90
Mutscher, Gus, 169

Nacogdoches, 19
Neches, battle of, 56
Neff, Governor Pat, 151, 156
Nimitz, Admiral Chester, 163, 164
Nolan, Philip (filibuster), 20

oil industry, 125-129, 154, 158-159, 165, 172
  offshore drilling controversy, 169
outlaws, 110-111, 162

Palo Duro Canyon, 2
Panhandle, 5
Parilla, Colonel, 18
People's Party, 122-123
Pease, Elisha M., 93, 95
Plum Creek, battle of, 56-57
politics and politicians, 120-122, 122-123, 137, 139-143, 169-172
Polk, President James K., 63, 64-65, 67
population of Texas, 1, 32, 62, 70, 110, 130, 139, 154, 167, 176
Prohibition, 149-150
Pueblos, 10-11

race relations, 94, 134-137, 139, 147, 151, 168, 174
Railroad Commission of 1891, 122
railroads, 113-116
Rainey, Homer Price, 168
Rayburn, Sam, 147, 159, 169-170
Reagan, John H., 122
Reconstruction era, 92-96
Red River, 3, 4-5
religion, 74
Republic of Texas, 43-44, 53-62
   annexation of with U.S., 61
   capital city of, 57
   declaration of, 43-44
   election of 1838, 54
   first election of (1836), 53-54
   flag of, 61-62
   foreign affairs of, 55-56
   Indian affairs of, 56-57
   population of, 62
   treaty with Mexico, 53
   under Sam Houston, 54, 58-59
Revolution from Mexico, 33, 35-52
Richards, Govenor Ann, 174
Rio Grande, 3, 6
roads. *See* transportation
Robinson, James W., 37
Roosevelt, President Franklin D., 159

Roosevelt, Theodore, 143-144
Rough Riders, 143-144
Rubí, Marquis de, 19

Sabine River, 3, 4
San Antonio (city), 12-15, 14-17, 35, 37-43, 58, 59, 73, 130, 147, 154, 167, 175
San Antonio de Valero. *See* Alamo
San Jacinto, battle of, 49-52
San José, Mission, 15, 16
San Juan, Mission, 17
San Sába, Mission, 18, 19
Santa Anna, General/President (Mexico), 28, 31, 37, 39, 40-41, 43, 44, 47, 49, 50, 51, 52, 53, 60, 69
Santa Fe Expedition, 55-56, 59
Sayers, Governor Joseph D., 140
schools. *See* education
Scott, General Winfield, 66, 67-69
Seguin, Juan, 39
settlers lives and views, 31-32, 71-72, 117
Sharp, Frank W., 169
Sharpstown, 169
Sheppard, Morris, 147
Sherman, General William Tecumseh, 104, 105
Sibley, General Henry H., 80-81
Signal Corps, 147
slavery, 69, 71, 72, 77, 78, 85-86, 92-93
Smith, Governor Henry, 33, 37, 54
Somervell, General Alexander, 59
Spanish-American War, 143-144
Spanish explorers and settlers, 10-12, 17-19
Spanish missionaries, 14, 17-19
Spindletop, 128-129
Stanford, Leland, 115
State Capitol Building (Austin), 123, 124
Sterling, Governor Ross, 158
Stevenson, Governor Coke R., 165

Sweatt, Herman, 168

Taylor, General Zachary, 64-66
Terán, Manuel Mier y, 28, 29
Texas fever, 97
Texas Preemption Act of 1854, 70
Texas Rangers, 54, 65-66, 106-107, 145
Throckmorton, James W., 93, 94
transportation, 72-73, 113-116
Travis, William Barrett, 29, 32, 38-39, 40-41
Treaty of Velasco, 53
Turtle Bay Resolutions, 29
Twiggs, General David, 79

Urrea, General (Mexican), 44, 47
USS Texas, 146, 147

Villa de San Fernando, 13

Walker, Ranger Samuel H., 60
Wallace, Ranger William A. A. "Big Foot", 31-32
Williams, Robert McAlpin, 25
Williams, Samuel May, 25
women's lives, about 71-72, 85, 148-149, 165, 174
women's suffrage movement, 148
World War I, 145, 147-148
World War II, 163-166

Yanaguana, 12

Zavala, Lorenzo de, 32, 37, 44

Discover the U.S.A. with State Illustrated Histories!

ARIZONA
Patrick Lavin
Patrick Lavin explores the Grand Canyon State, a "land of contrasts" whose history is as varied and fascinating as its landscapes. No other North American region offers such environmental diversity, including the native plants, animals, and people that inhabit it. Complemented by over 60 photographs and maps, this concise history recounts the story of Arizona from the prehistoric days of the Paleo-Indians to the twenty-first century.
252 pages • ISBN 0-7818-0852-9 • $14.95pb

CALIFORNIA
Robert J. Chandler
Thirty-six million Americans (and counting) live in California, more than any other state. Robert J. Chandler's sweeping history begins with the area's indigenous inhabitants, and leads through the era of Spanish colonization, conquest by the United States, the gold rush, the founding of Hollywood, and modern developments like Silicon Valley. Always the trendsetter, California remains prominent in both America's and the world's culture and economy.
252 pages • ISBN 0-7818-1034-5 • $14.95pb

FLORIDA
Robert A. Taylor
From Spanish conquistadors to Jeb Bush, the grand history of Florida is presented here with over 50 illustrations, photographs, and maps. Florida has the longest history of any state, dating back to the Spanish conquistadors in the early sixteenth century. From the voyages of Ponce de León to the dawn of the Space Age, the jewel of the Sunbelt has played an important role in the history of the United States. This concise history chronicles the struggles between the United States and Spain, the trauma of the Civil War, and the ways Floridians have grappled with the problems of over-development in the "Sunshine State." Perfect for the vacationer, the student and the curious reader.
238 pages • ISBN 0-7818-1052-3 • $14.95pb

MISSOURI
Sean McLachlan
Originally part of the Louisiana Purchase and nicknamed 'The Gateway to the West' because it was as departure point for Westward-bound settlers, Missouri became a state in 1821. This is a lively and thorough account of Missouri's exciting and pivotal role in history—from the first Native American inhabitants to the territorial period, from the agony of the Civil War to the freewheeling jazz and Prohibition eras, from labor and civil rights struggles to the triumph of the St. Louis Arch. Descriptions of these tumultuous and glorious times come from the diaries, newspaper articles, journals and letters of ordinary Missourians—reporters, soldiers, merchants and wives who pro-

vide first-person testimony to the march of history. Over 50 photographs of leading figures and events, maps, a time line and illustrations bring the past vividly to life in this history of the 'Show-Me' state.
249 pages • ISBN 0-7818-1196-1 • $14.95pb

NEW MEXICO
Patrick Lavin
New Mexico's history is as varied and intriguing as its magnificent landscapes. Archaeological evidence shows that the area was the site of a prehistoric civilization that may have been the oldest in North America. In later times, three cultures—Native Americans, Spanish, and Anglo—coexisted there. Throughout New Mexico's territorial period, desperados and cattle rustling led to colorful tales of conflict. The state's natural beauty and rich cultural life, from Carlsbad Caverns National Park to the historic pueblos of Taos, continue to draw visitors to this day. Complemented by over 50 illustrations, photographs, and maps, this history of New Mexico is a concise yet comprehensive chronicle of the state. Travelers, students, and readers interested in the Southwest will find it an ideal resource.
253 pages • ISBN 0-7818-1053-1 • $14.95pb

PENNSYLVANIA
Donald E. Markle
Originally settled by Swedes, Pennsylvania became the single largest land grant to an individual in history when Charles II of England signed it over to William Penn in 1681. The transaction never turned a profit for Penn, but proved fateful—the colony quickly evolved into a nucleus of American politics, culture, and social reform. Complemented by 50 photographs, illustrations, and maps, this concise volume begins with the history of Pennsylvania from the Native American era to colonial times, when Philadelphia served as the birthplace and first capital of a new nation. It then moves through the centuries to explore the oil, coal, iron, and steel industries that developed in the nineteenth century, ending with an overview of modern-day Pennsylvania.
210 pages • ISBN 0-7818-1197-X • $14.95pb

VIRGINIA
Deborah Welch
Named for the "Virgin Queen" Elizabeth I, the Commonwealth of Virginia has played an important role in American history. In 1607, Jamestown became the first permanent English colony, and after the Revolutionary War, four of the first five presidents were Virginians. Today, four more Virginians have served as Commander in Chief and its proximity to the capital has maintained its role in government, including being home to the CIA headquarters, the Pentagon, the FBI Academy and the Quantico Marine Corp Base. With over 60 photographs, illustrations and maps, Welch takes readers through a concise, intriguing look at one of the four commonwealths.
220 pages • ISBN 0-7818-1115-5 • $14.95pb

U.S. Travel Guides

Long Island: A Guide to New York's Suffolk and Nassau Counties
Raymond Spinzia, Judith Spinzia, and Kathryn Spinzia Rayne

"*A family collaboration that will prove indispensible both to Long Island visitors and long-time residents.*" —Long Island Historical Journal

Known for its beautiful beaches, fishing villages, quaint towns and world-famous wineries, Long Island welcomes thousands of visitors every year. This edition of the first comprehensive guidebook to the island has been completely revised and updated. Organized by town, the guide provides 578 entries, including 135 new ones, invaluable practical information such as driving directions and maps, a catalog of Tiffany stained-glass windows in Suffolk and Nassau counties, and lists of wineries and Gold Coast mansions that can be visited or rented.

408 pages • ISBN 0-7818-1213-5 • $14.95pb

Discover Native America: Arizona, Colorado, New Mexico and Utah
Expanded Edition
Tish Minear and Janet Limon

This newly expanded edition of the popular Hippocrene travel guide highlights the prehistoric cultures of Arizona, Colorado, New Mexico, and Utah, as well as the modern tribes that now live in these spectacular "Four Corners" states. Arranged geographically, the guide includes information on the Navajo, Apache, Ute, Tohono O'odham, Pueblo, Hopi, and more, with a calendar of powwows and other tribal ceremonies, tips on visiting reservations, and dozens of new sites and place to stay, eat and shop. With a glossary of useful words and phrases in several Native American languages, maps and a 16-page color photo insert, this is a unique companion for Southwest adventures.

482 pages • ISBN 0-7818-1198-8 • $24.95pb

The Navajo Nation: A Visitor's Guide
Patrick and Joan Lavin

The Navajo are the largest Native American tribe in the United States, with their land spanning 25,000 square miles. This unique guidebook is divided into three sections: a history of the Diné, a geographical visitor's guide, and an introduction to the Navajo language. It includes attractions, routes, dining options, and accommodations with suggested itineraries for 3-day to 10-day trips, with special details for RVs, camping, and hiking. A 16-page color photo insert brings Navajo country to life.

282 pages • ISBN 0-7818-1180-5 • $21.95pb

Prices subject to change without prior notice. To purchase **Hippocrene Books** contact your local bookstore, visit www.hippocrenebooks.com, call (212) 685-4373, or write to: HIPPOCRENE BOOKS, 171 Madison Avenue, New York, NY 10016.